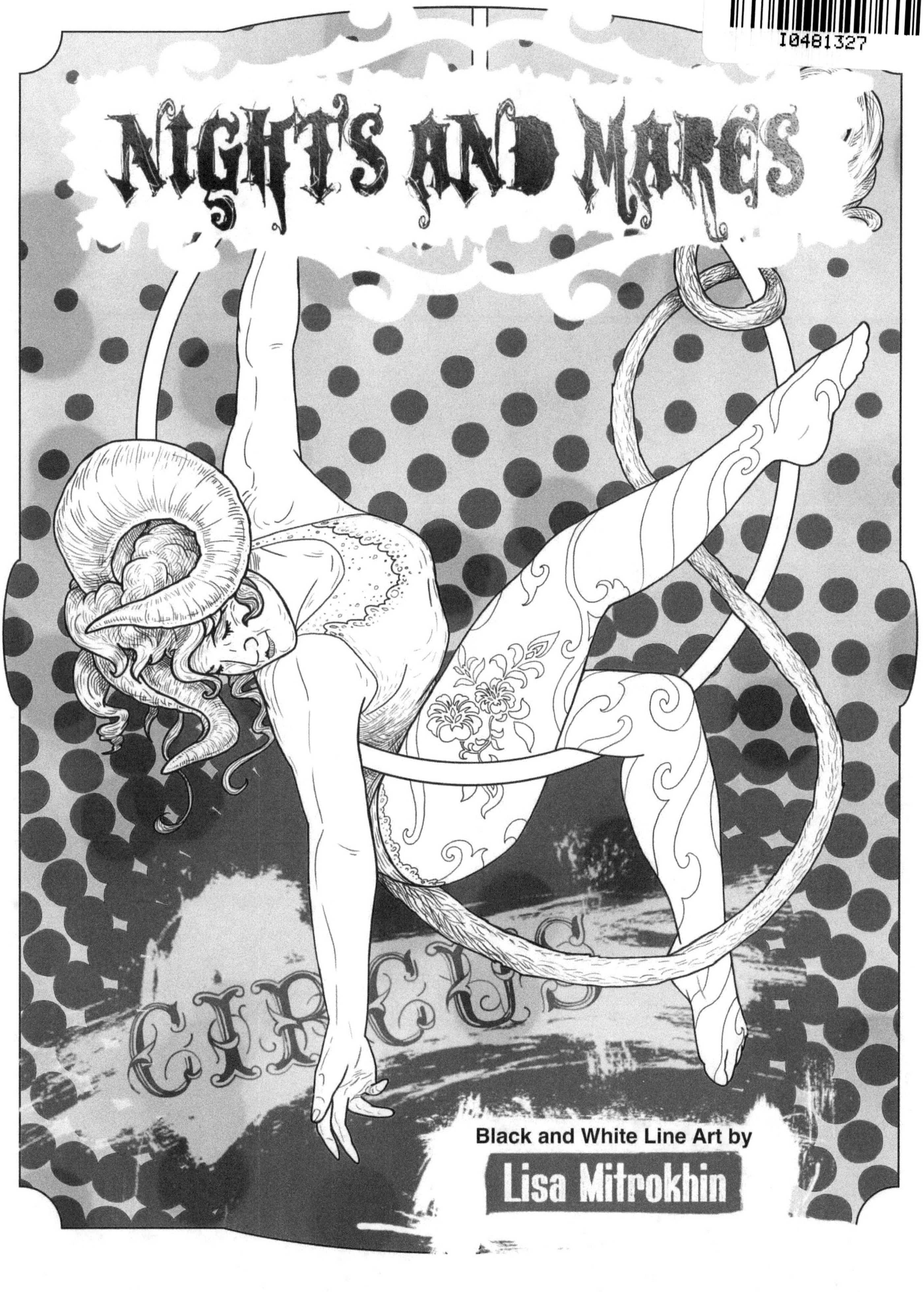

NIGHT'S AND MARES

Black and White Line Art by

Lisa Mitrokhin

WELCOME

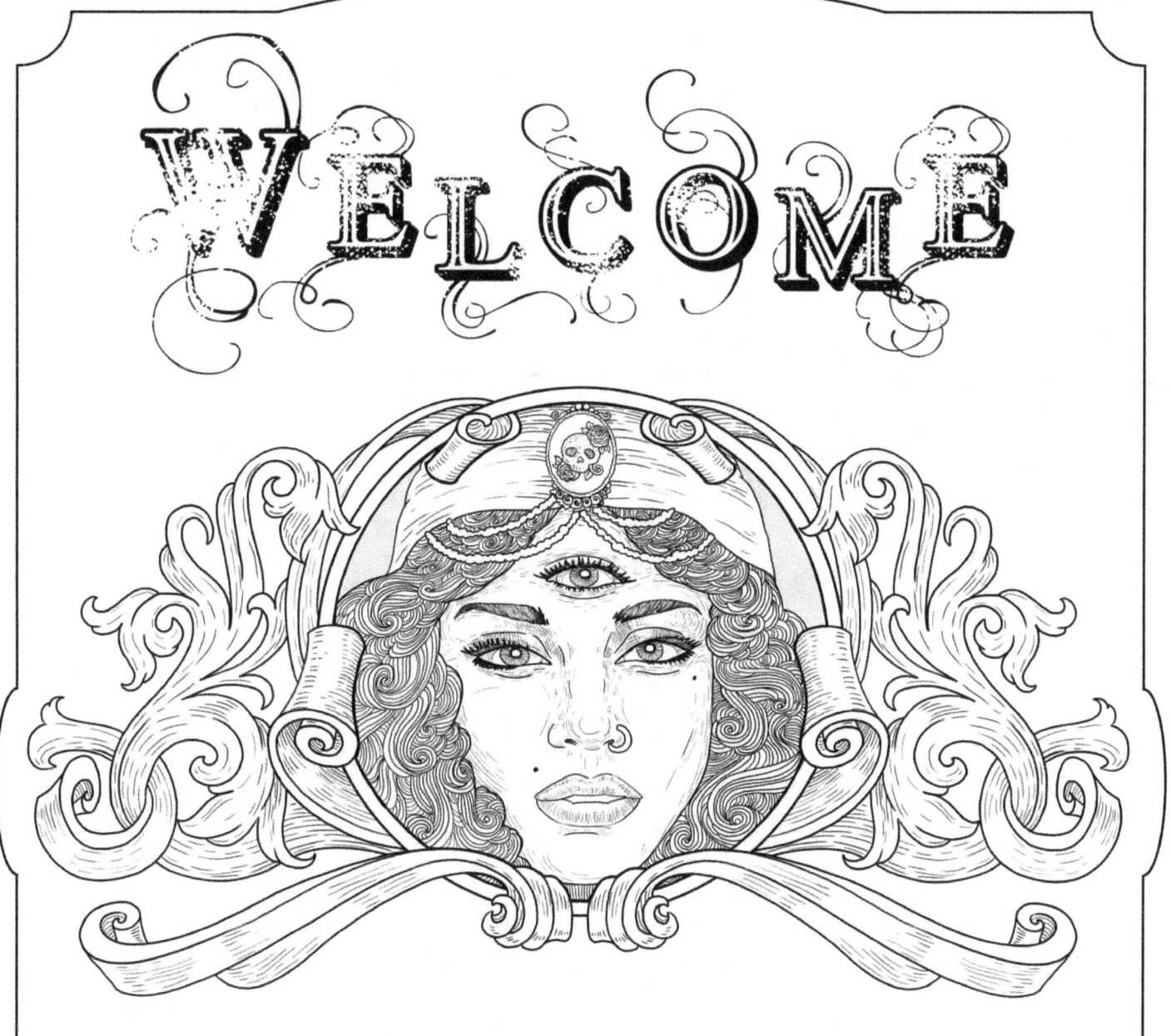

ENJOY THE SHOW

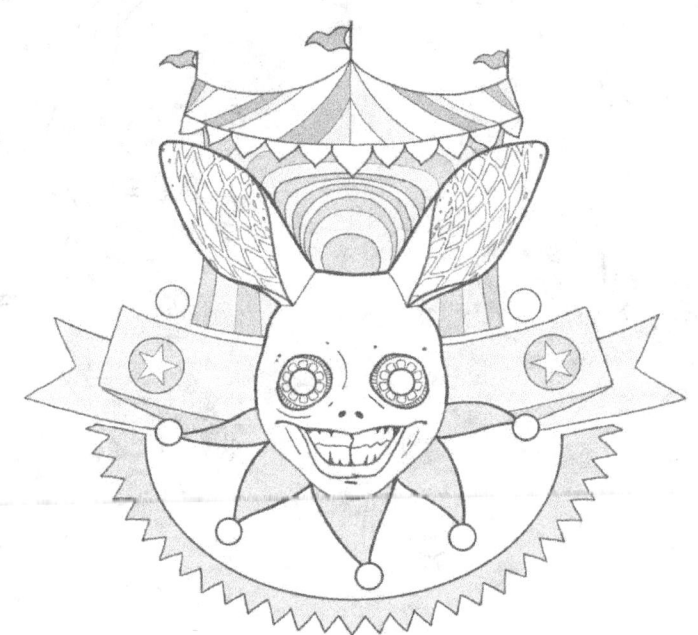

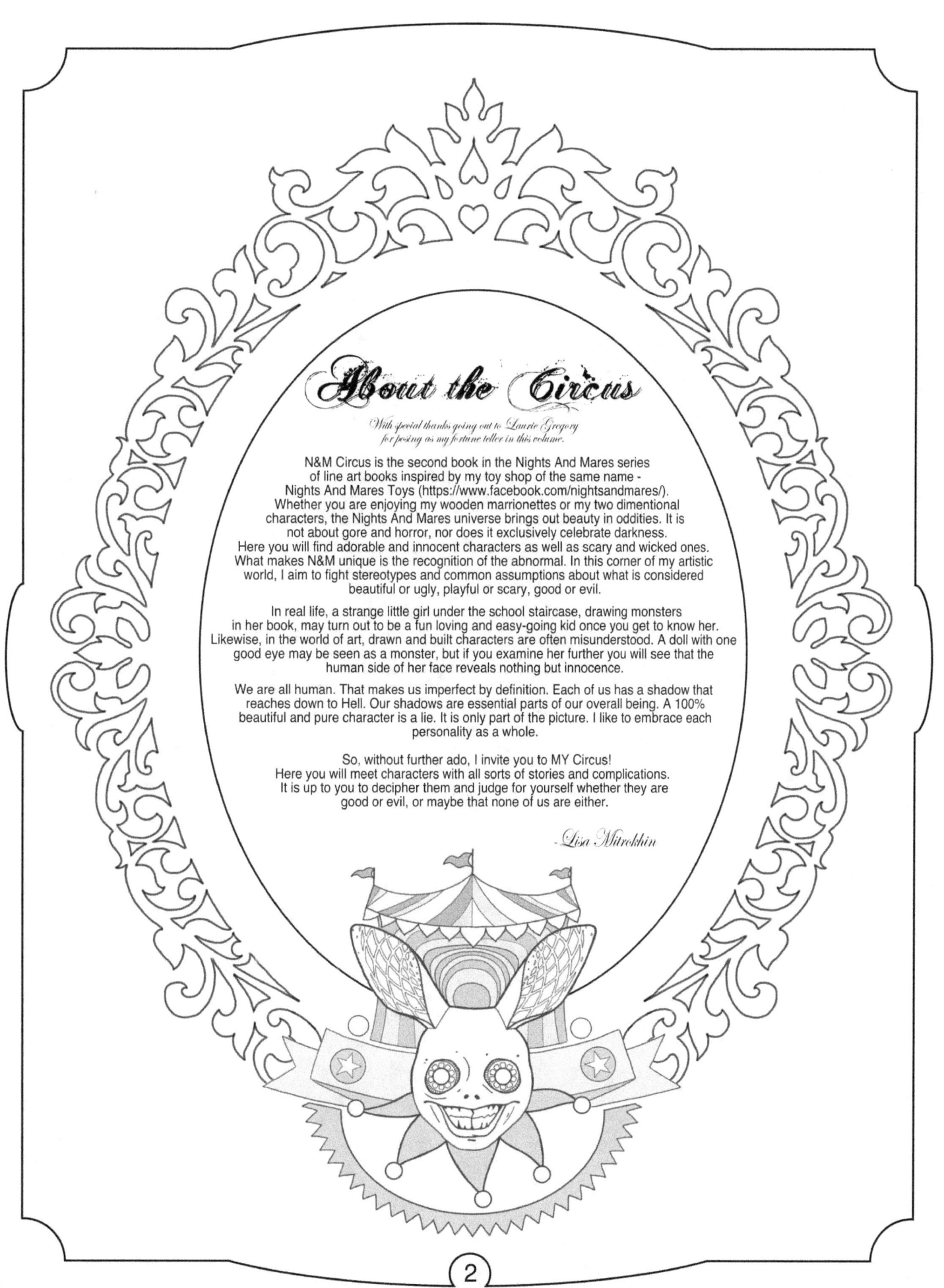

About the Circus

*With special thanks going out to Laurie Gregory
for posing as my fortune teller in this volume.*

N&M Circus is the second book in the Nights And Mares series
of line art books inspired by my toy shop of the same name -
Nights And Mares Toys (https://www.facebook.com/nightsandmares/).
Whether you are enjoying my wooden marrionettes or my two dimentional
characters, the Nights And Mares universe brings out beauty in oddities. It is
not about gore and horror, nor does it exclusively celebrate darkness.
Here you will find adorable and innocent characters as well as scary and wicked ones.
What makes N&M unique is the recognition of the abnormal. In this corner of my artistic
world, I aim to fight stereotypes and common assumptions about what is considered
beautiful or ugly, playful or scary, good or evil.

In real life, a strange little girl under the school staircase, drawing monsters
in her book, may turn out to be a fun loving and easy-going kid once you get to know her.
Likewise, in the world of art, drawn and built characters are often misunderstood. A doll with one
good eye may be seen as a monster, but if you examine her further you will see that the
human side of her face reveals nothing but innocence.

We are all human. That makes us imperfect by definition. Each of us has a shadow that
reaches down to Hell. Our shadows are essential parts of our overall being. A 100%
beautiful and pure character is a lie. It is only part of the picture. I like to embrace each
personality as a whole.

So, without further ado, I invite you to MY Circus!
Here you will meet characters with all sorts of stories and complications.
It is up to you to decipher them and judge for yourself whether they are
good or evil, or maybe that none of us are either.

Lisa Mitrokhin

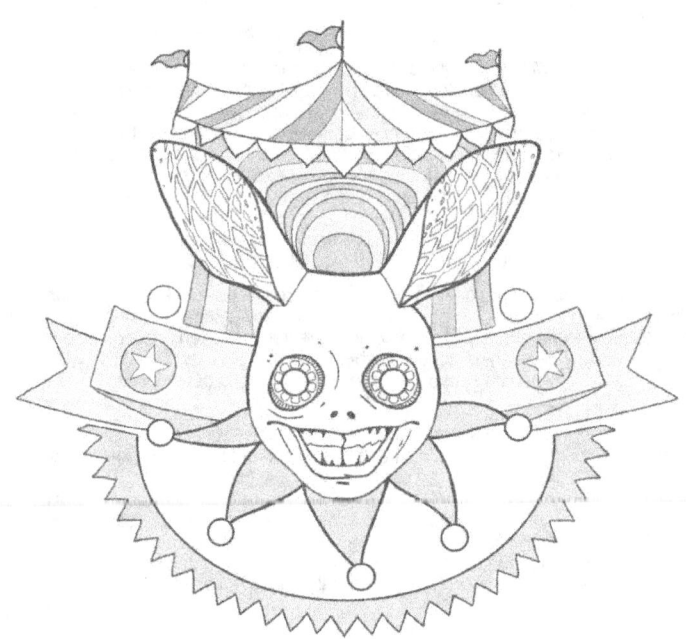

TABLE OF CONTENTS

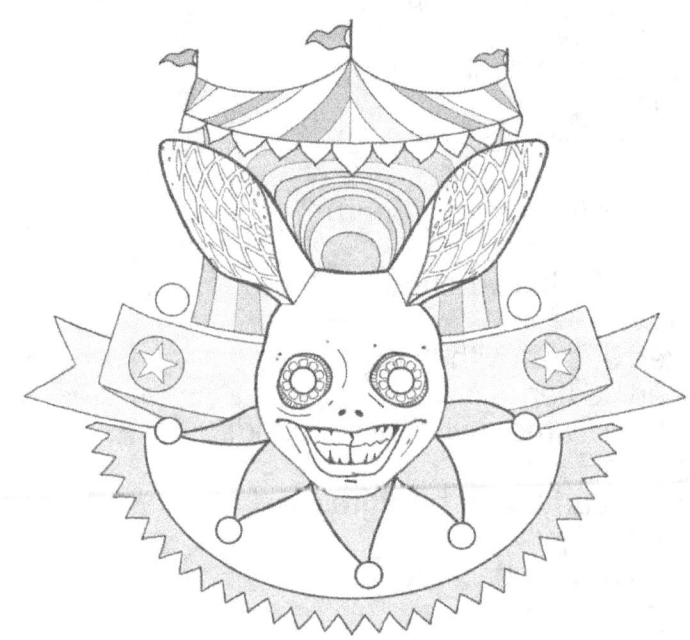

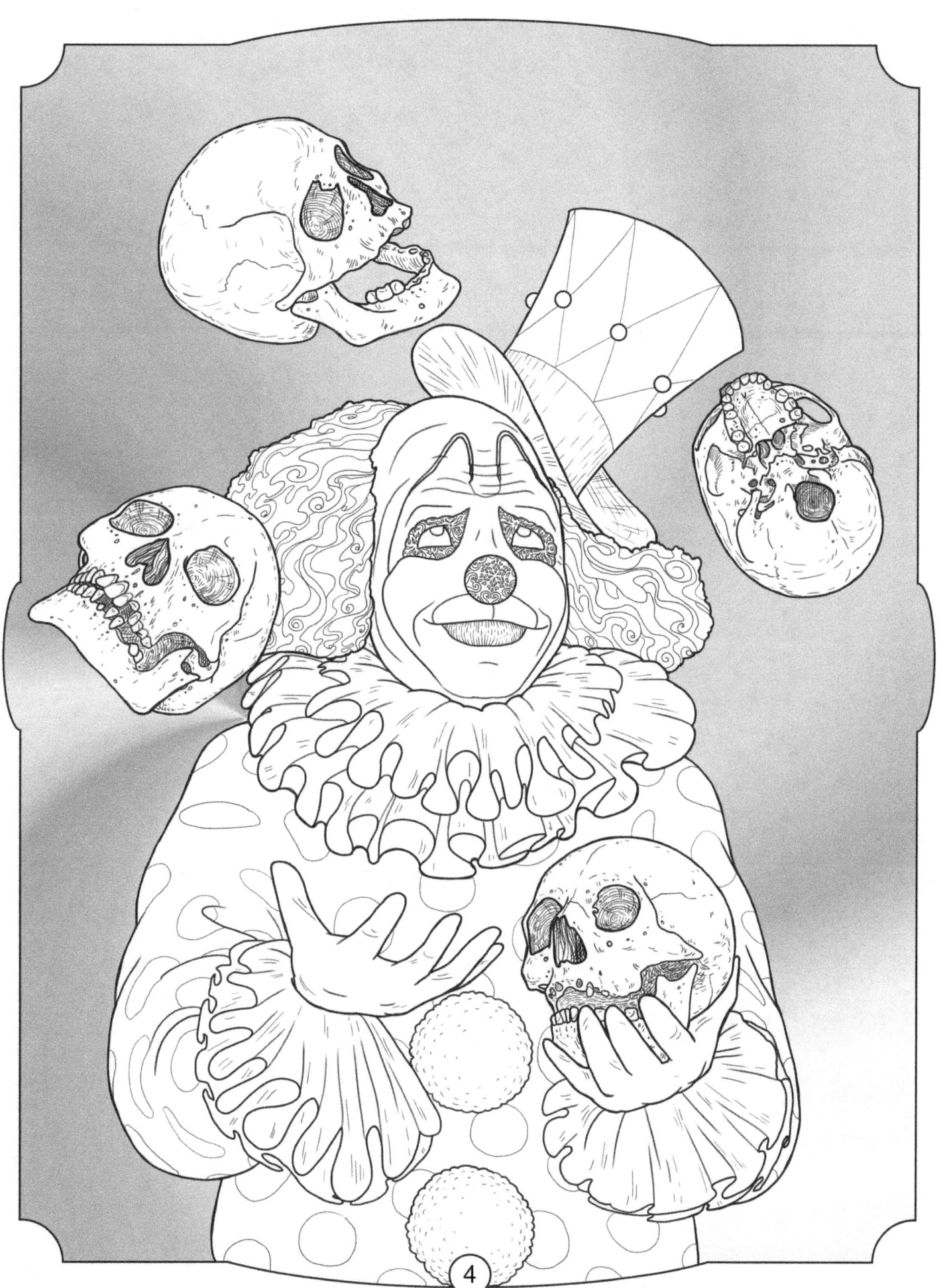

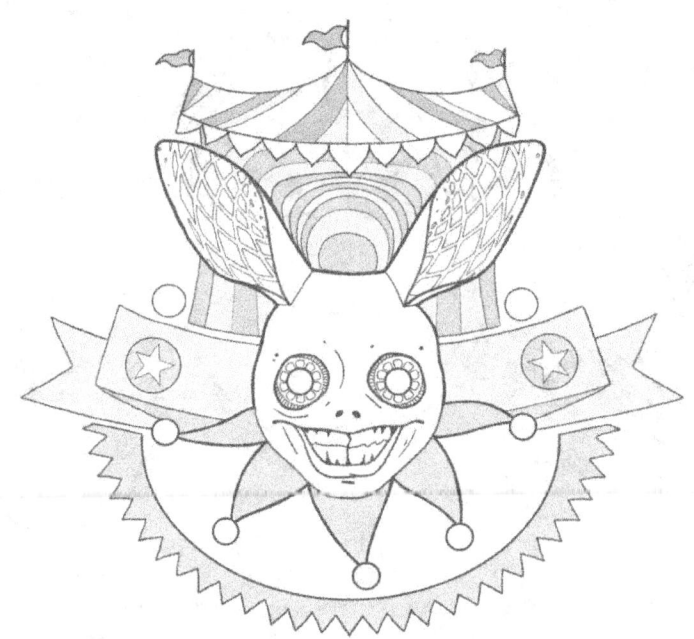

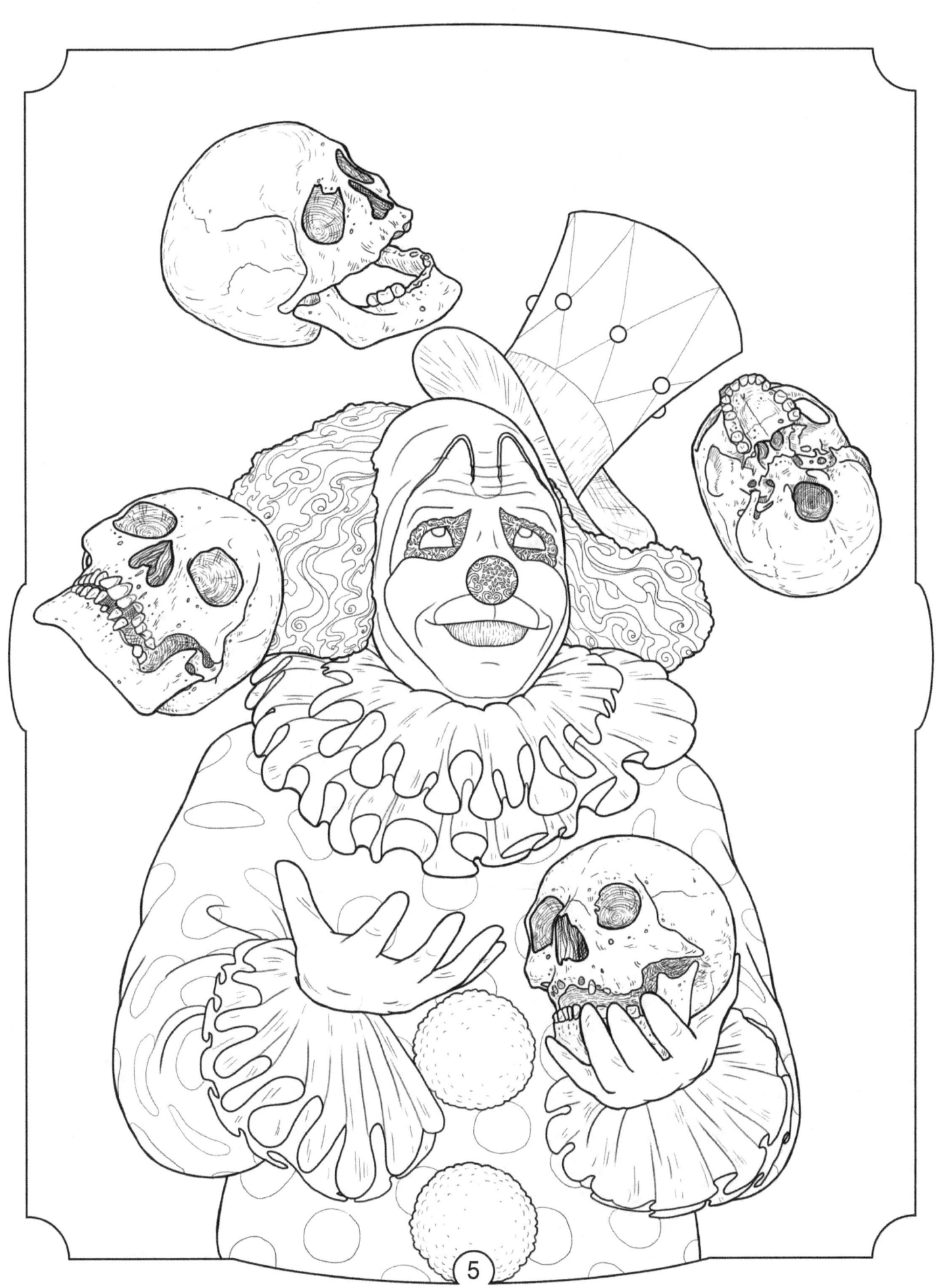

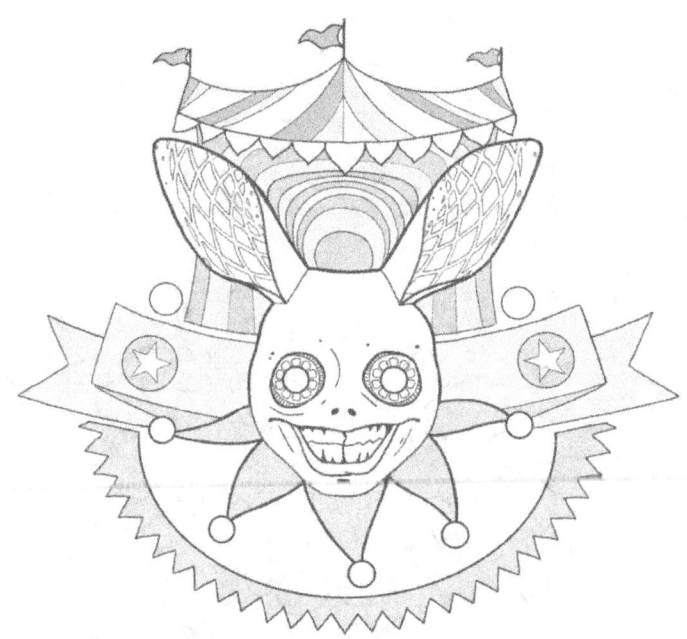

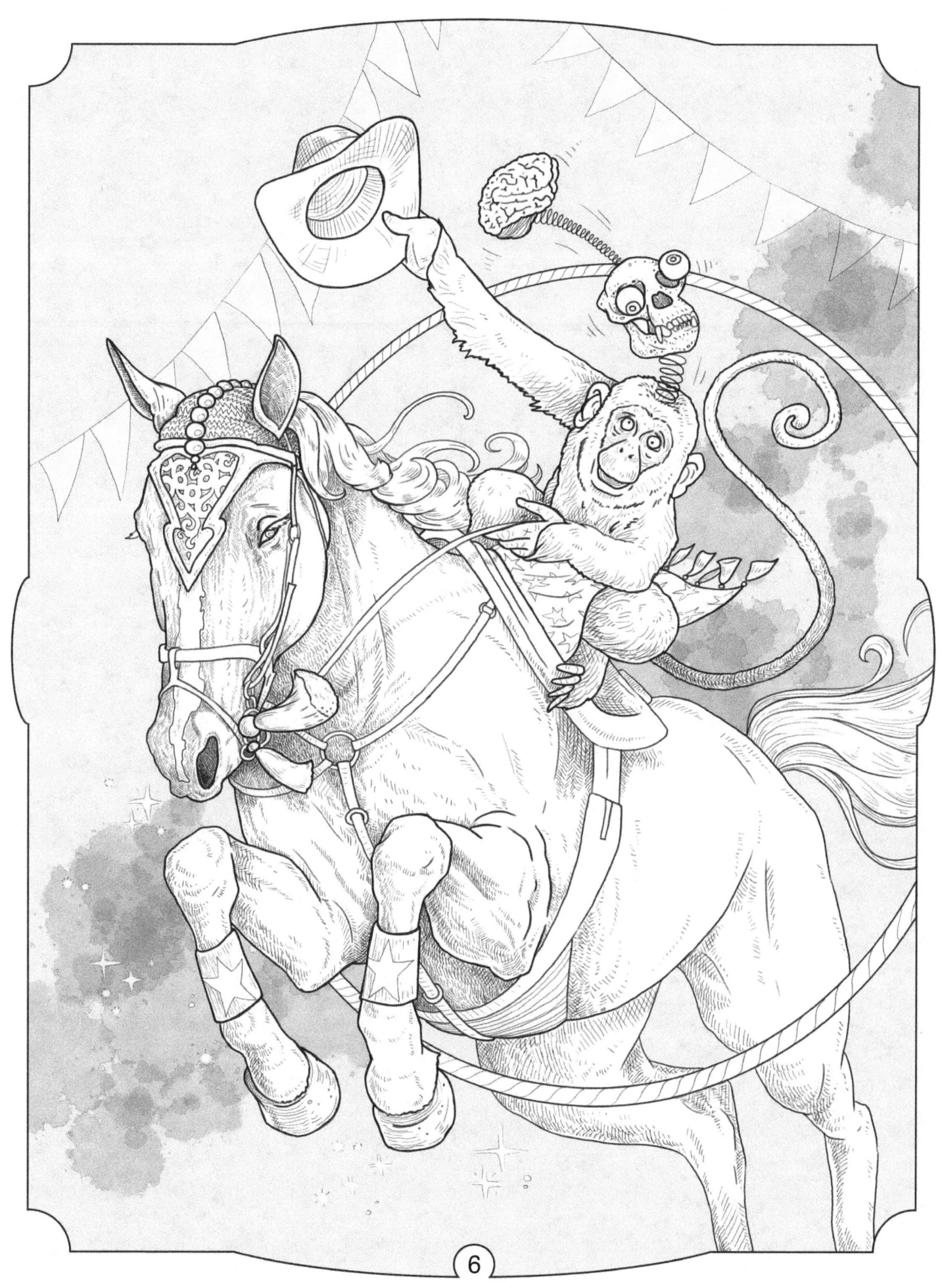

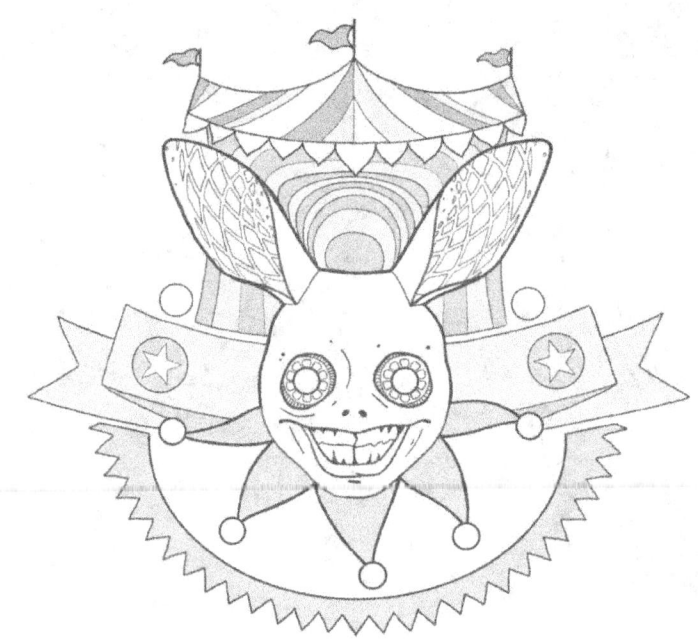

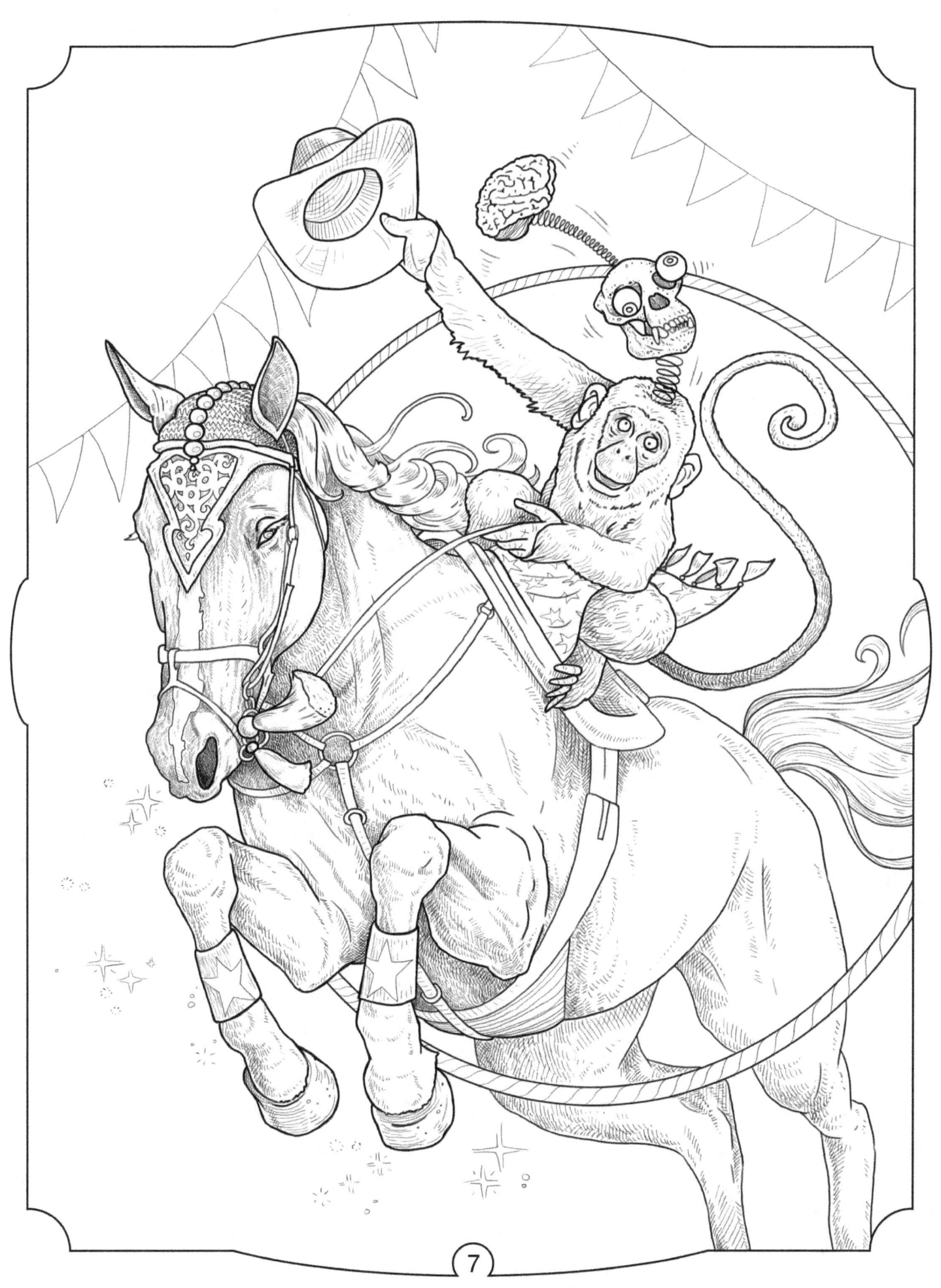

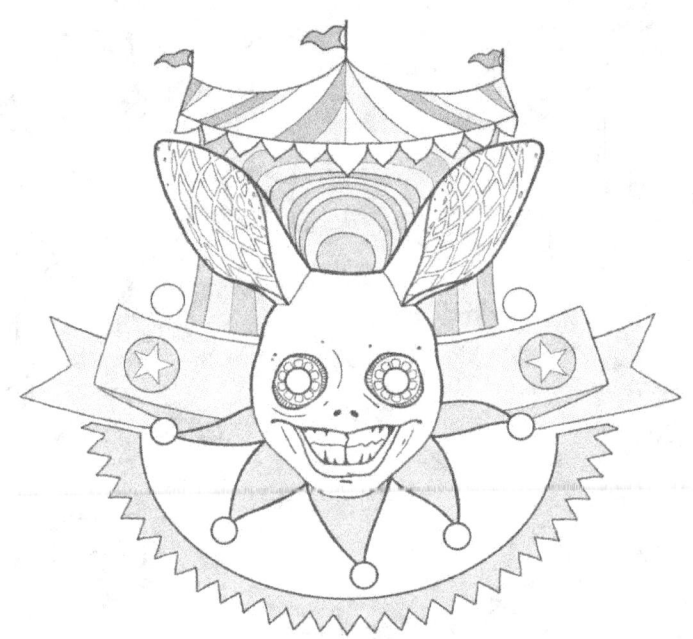

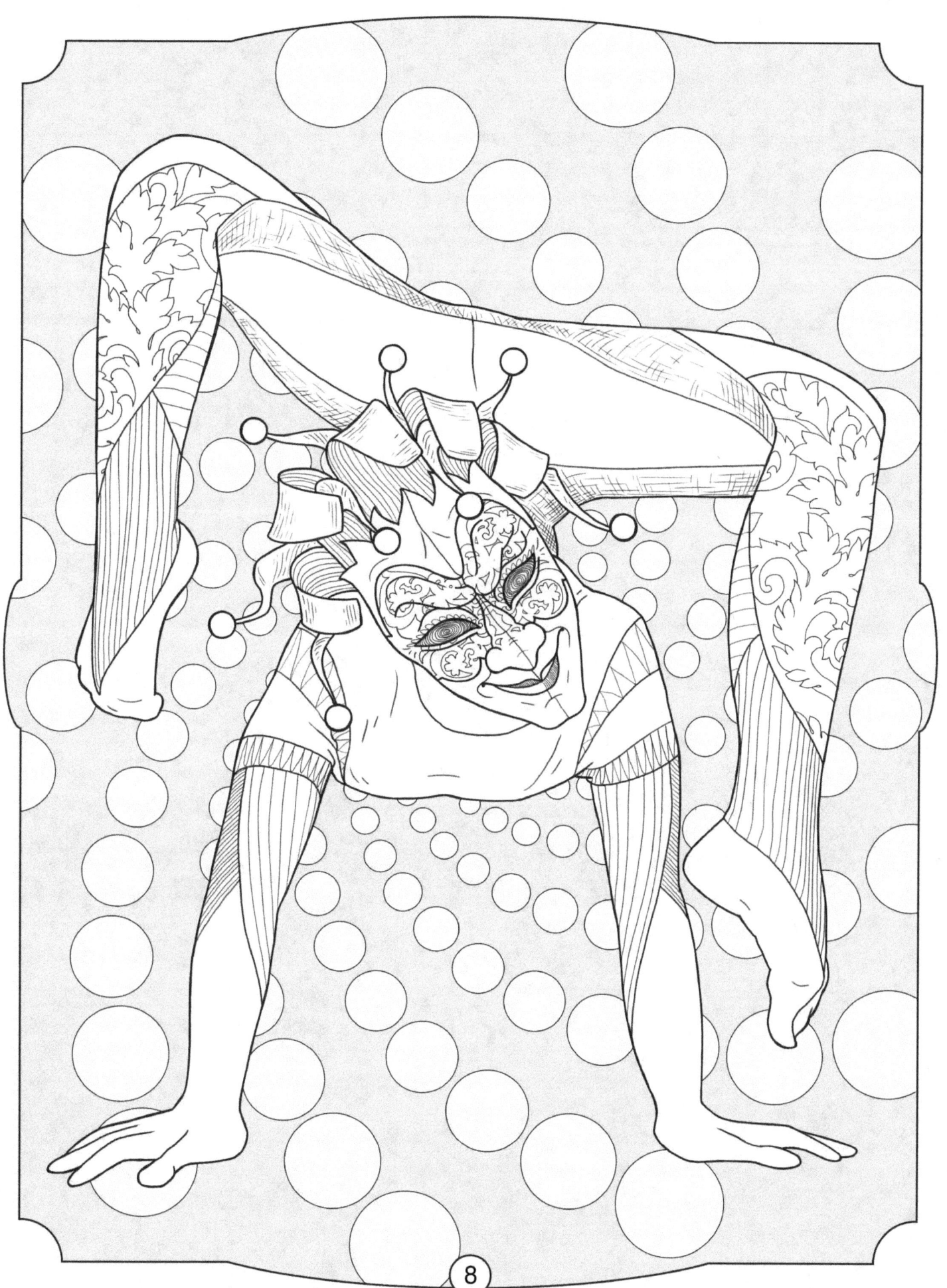

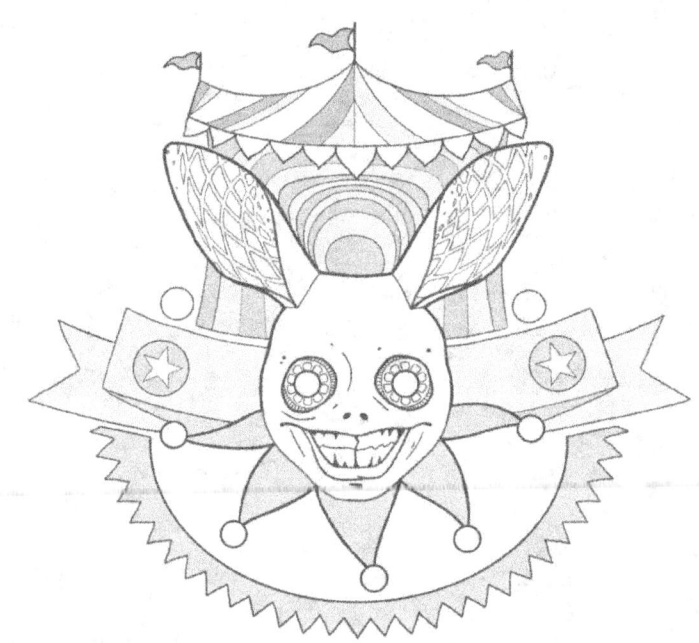

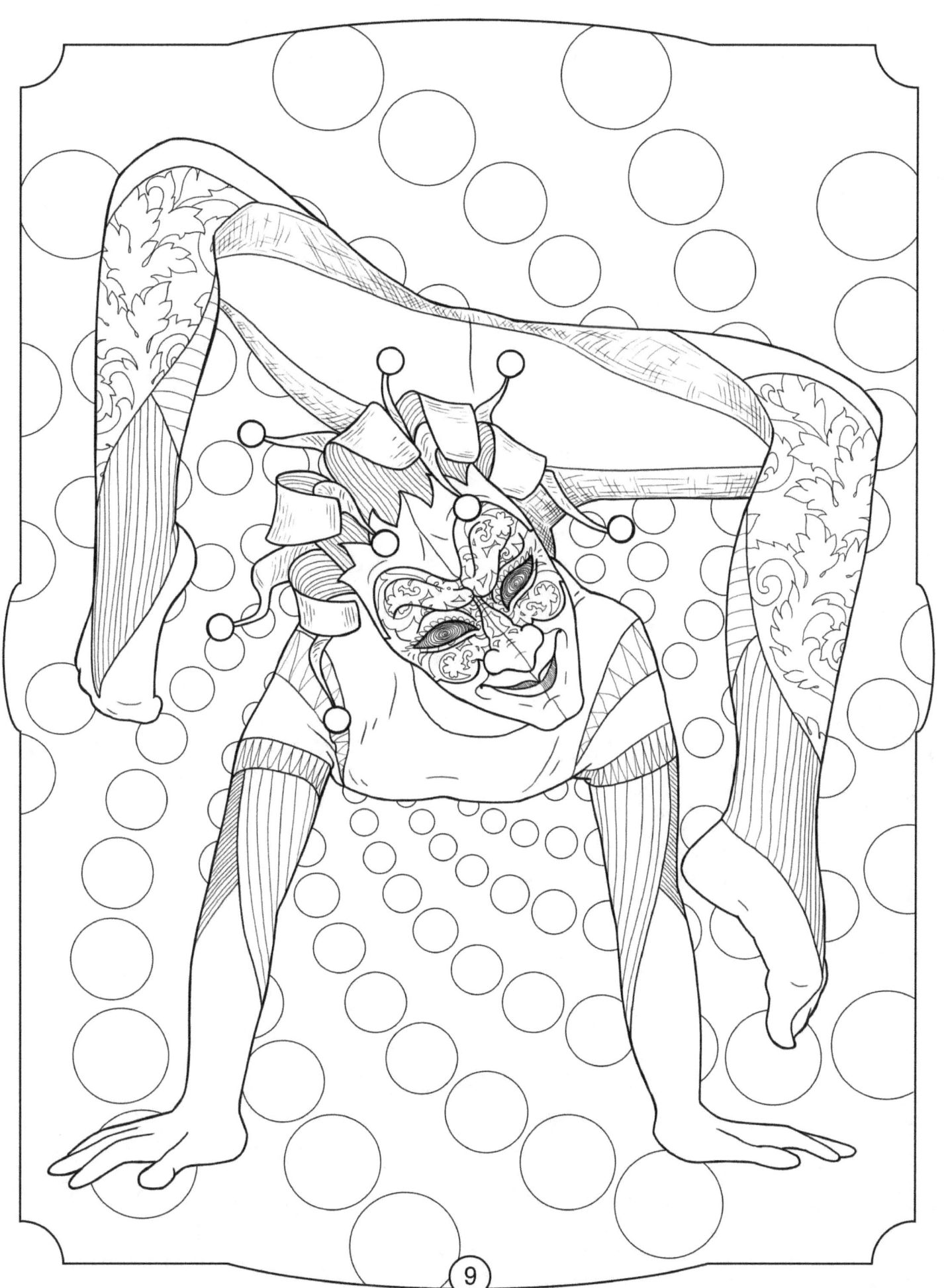

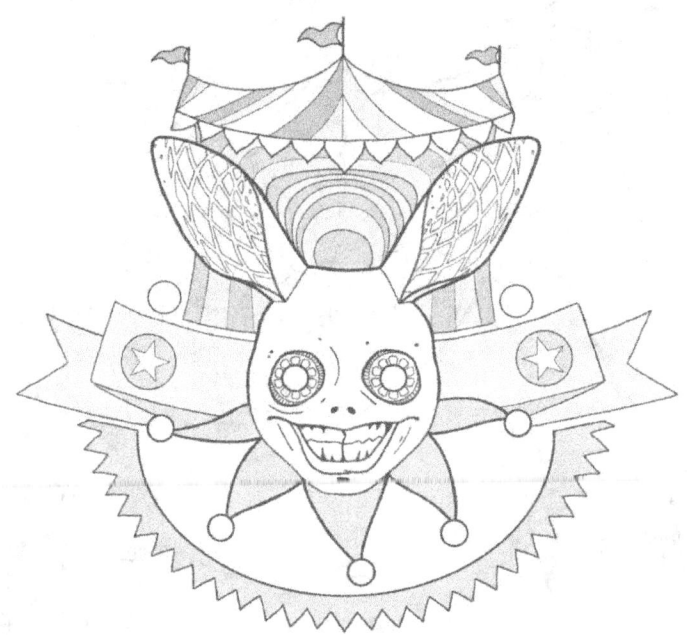

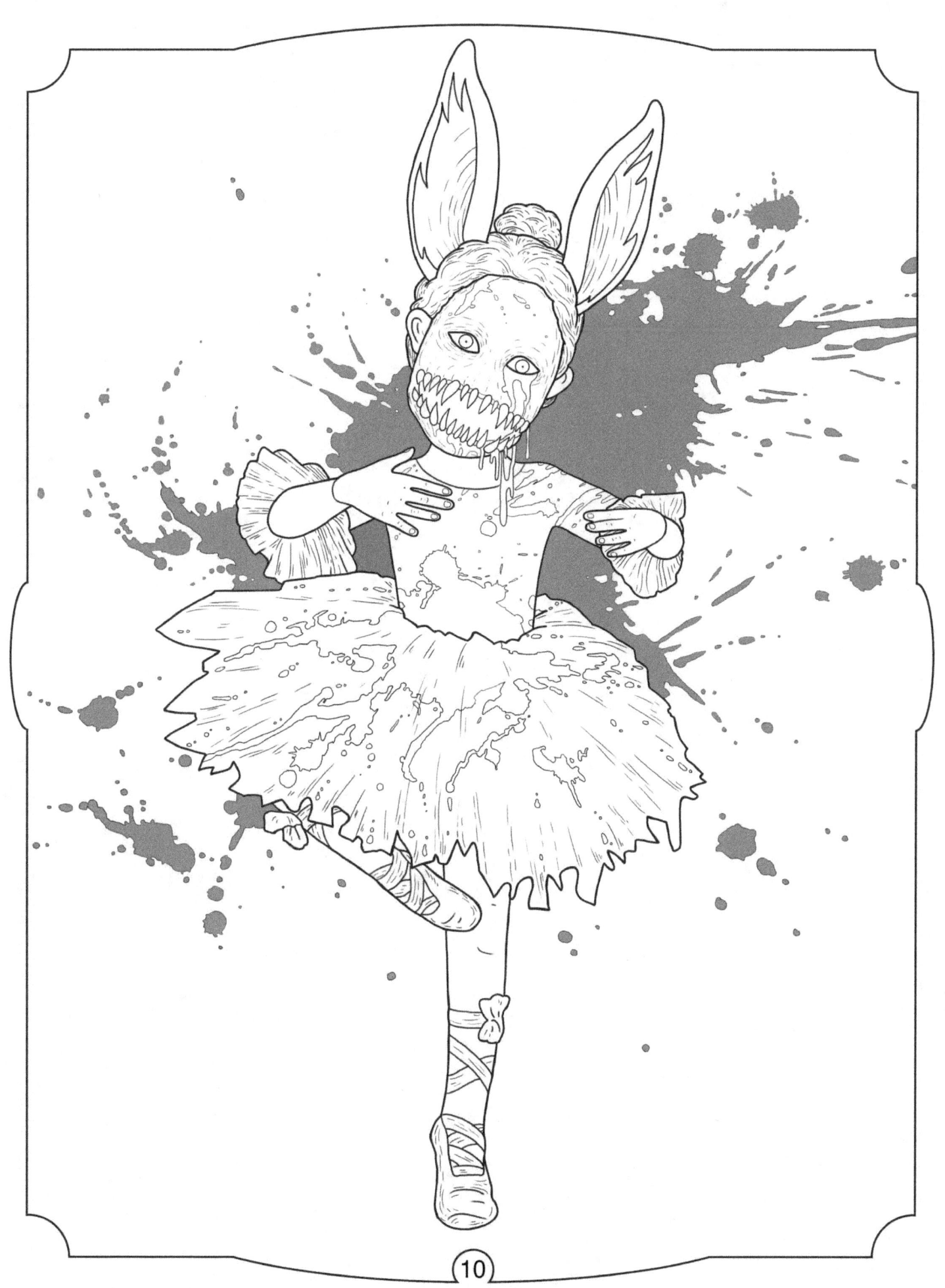

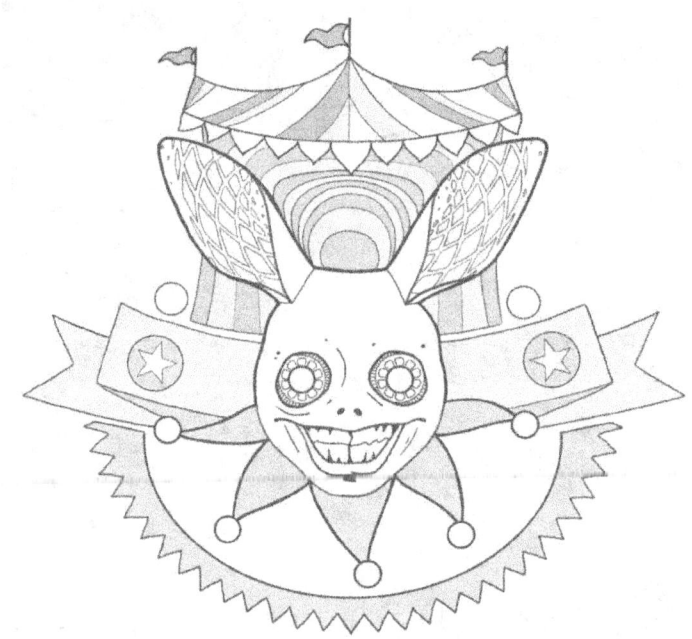

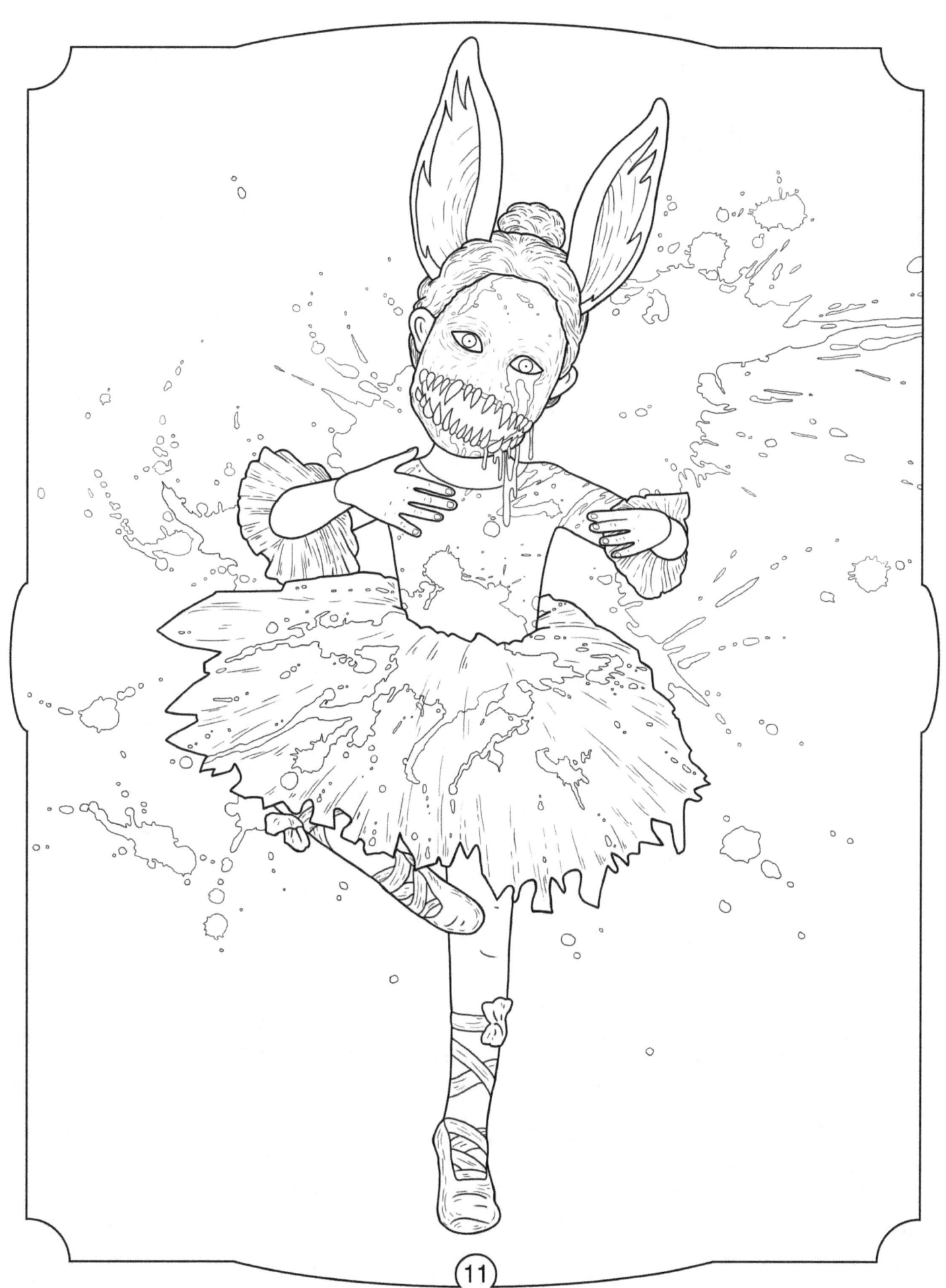

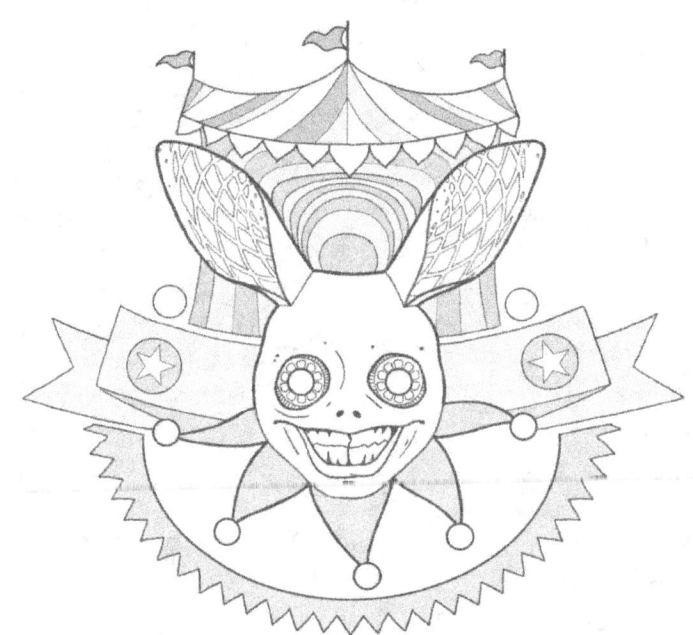

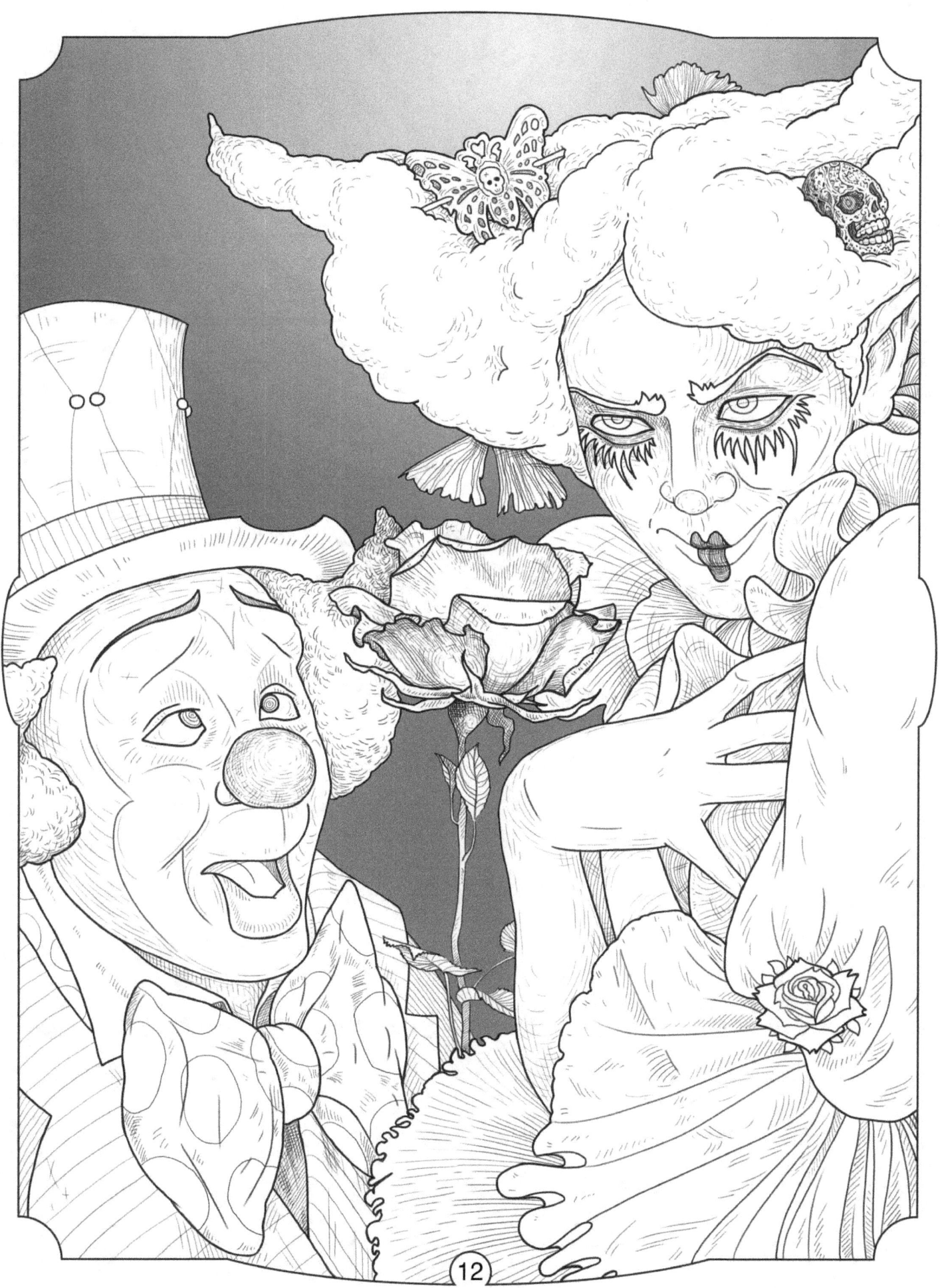

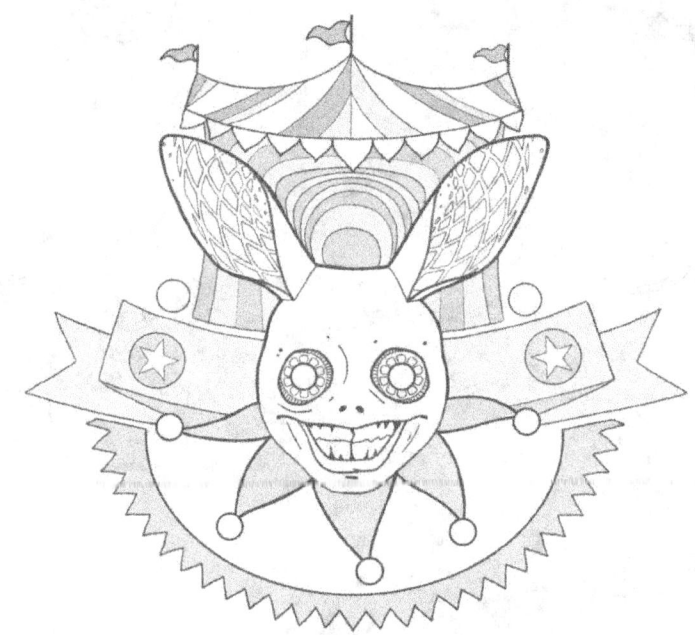

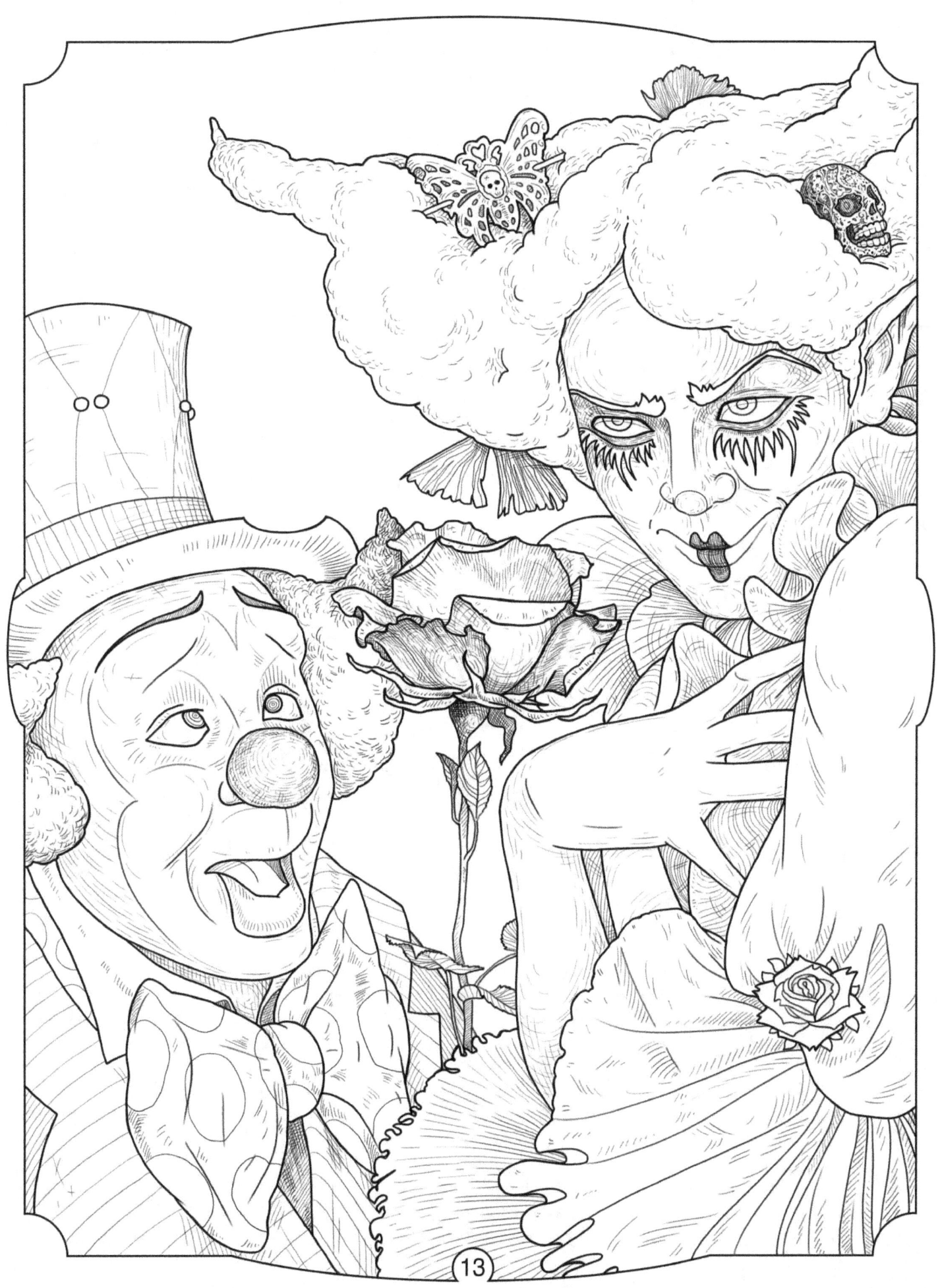

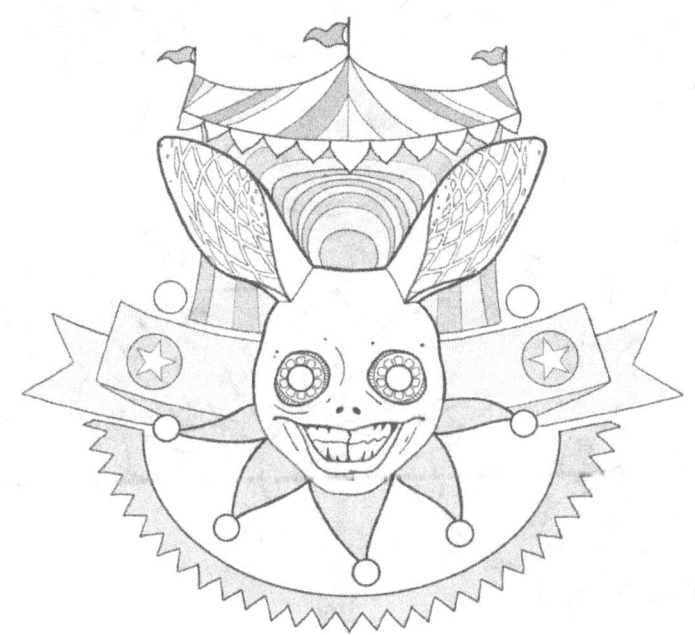

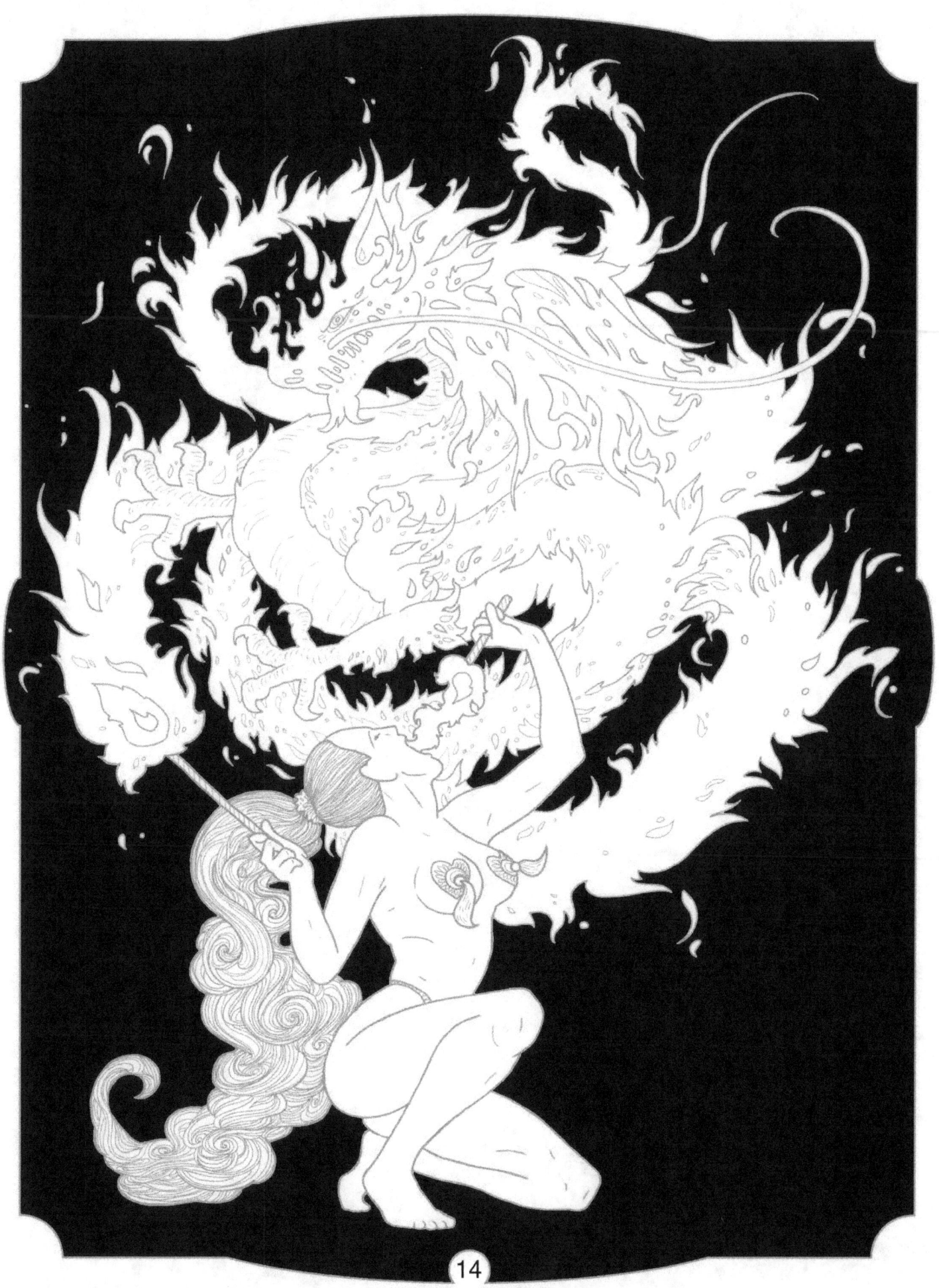

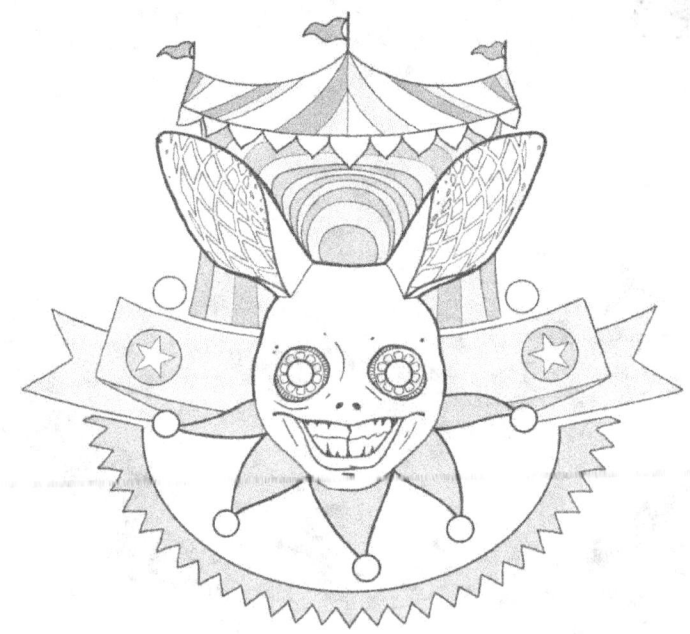

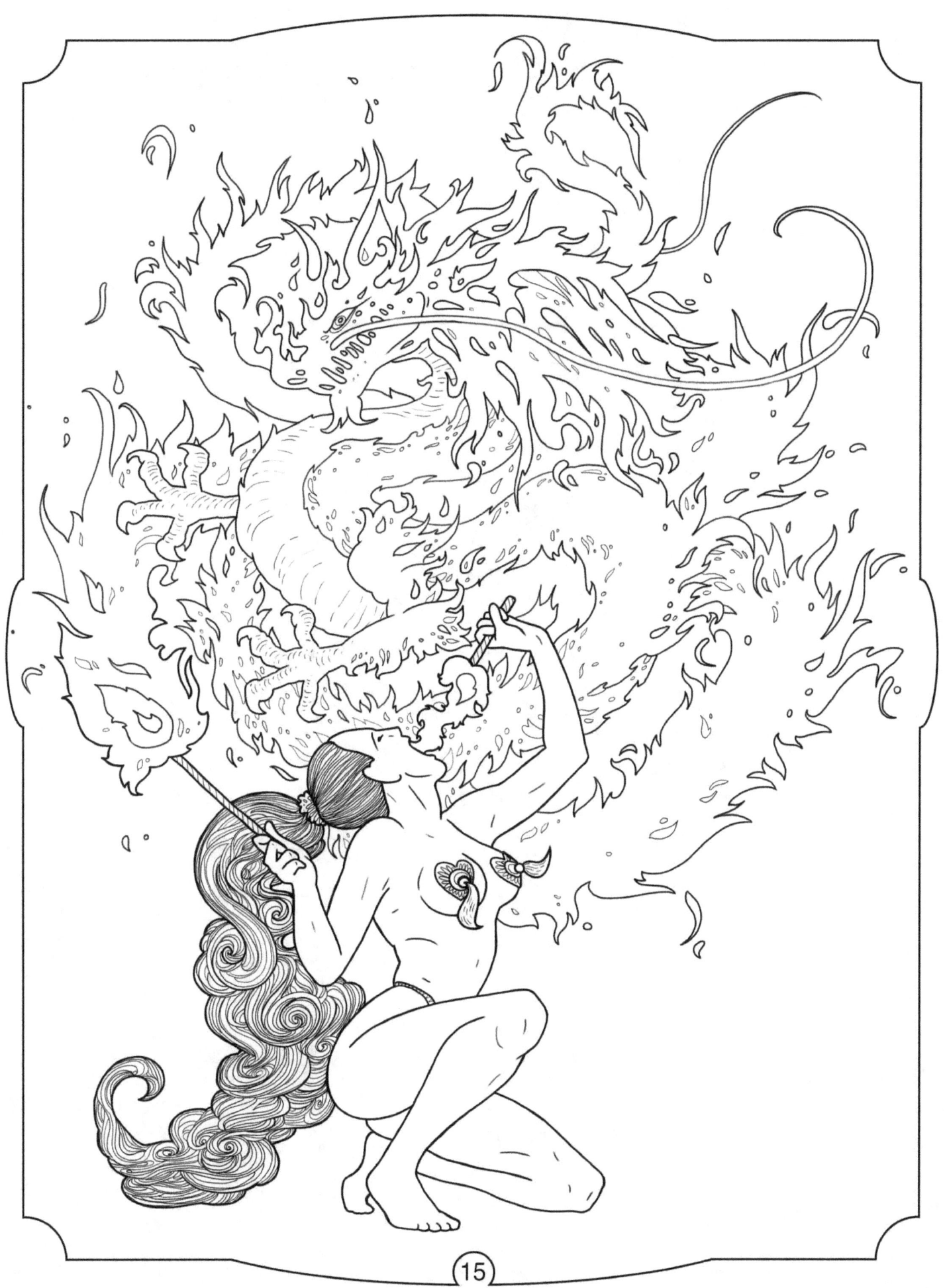

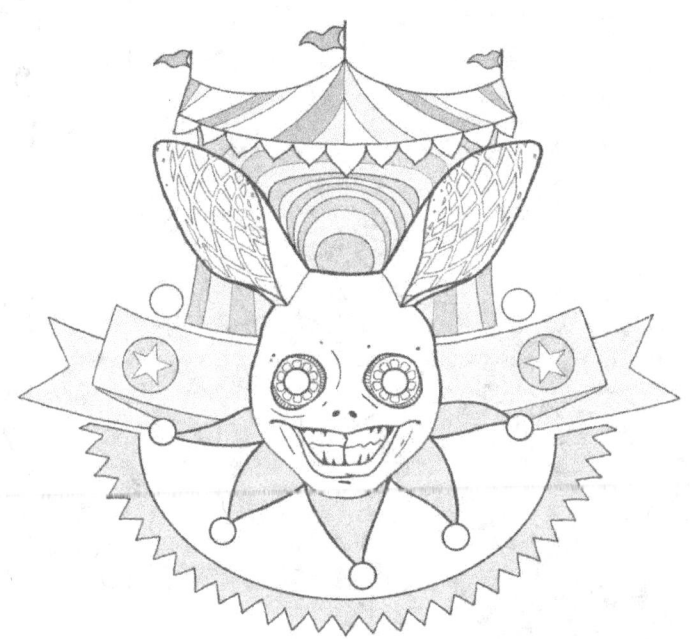

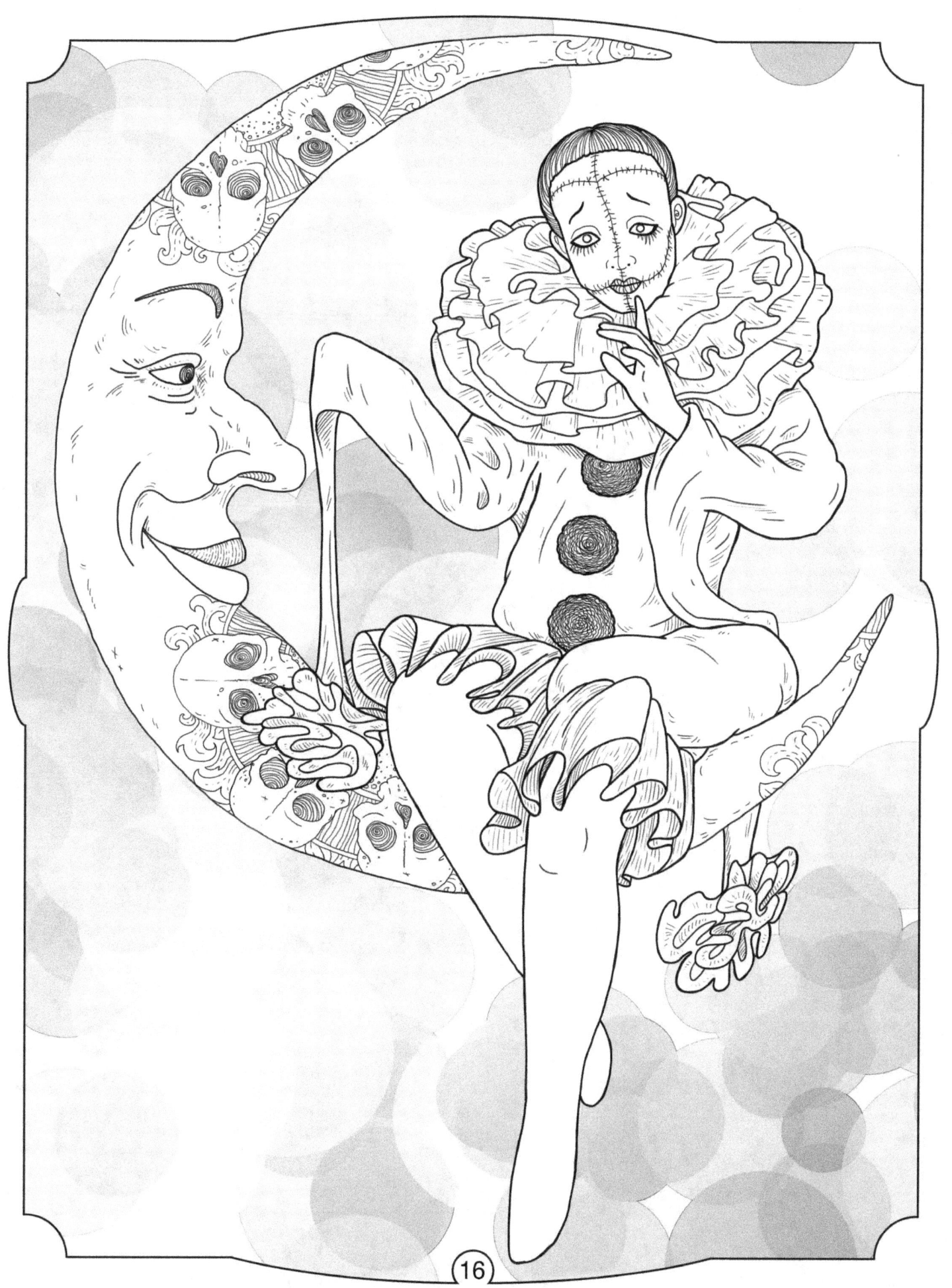

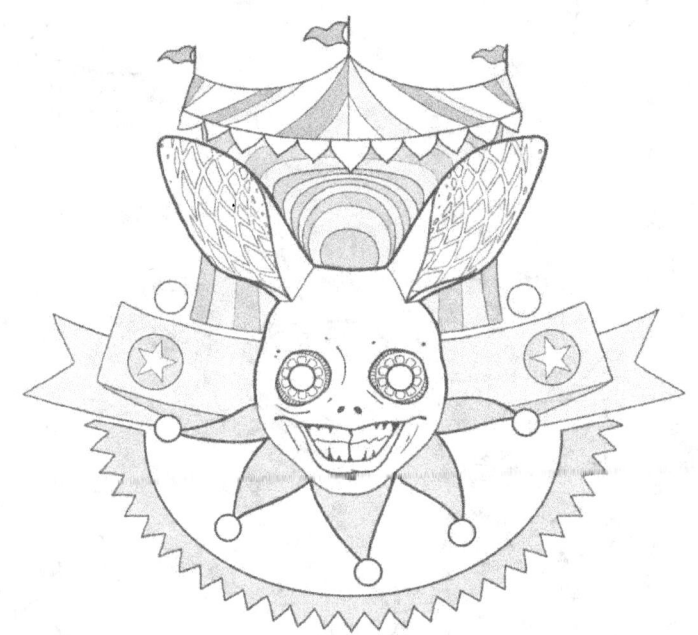

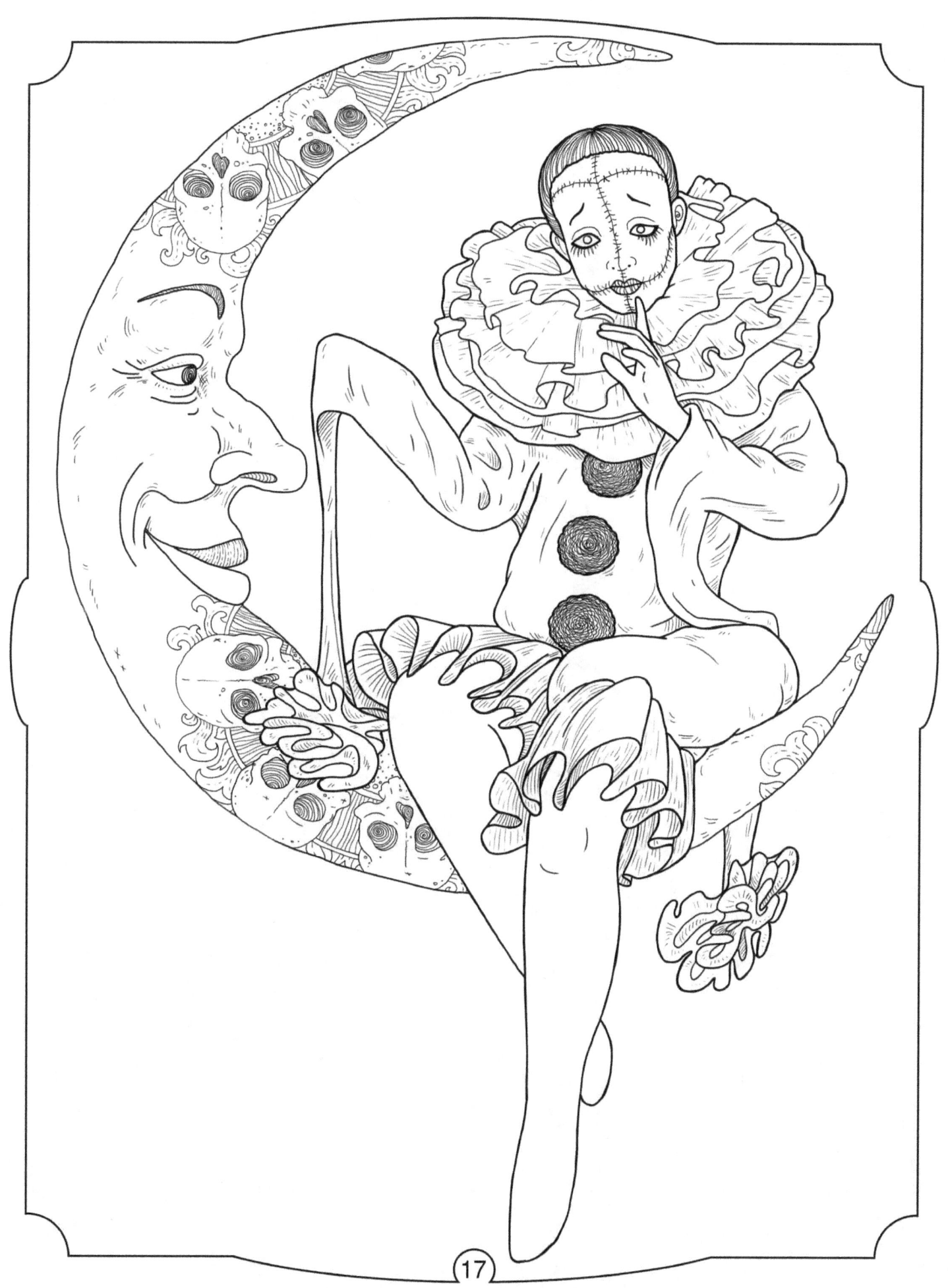

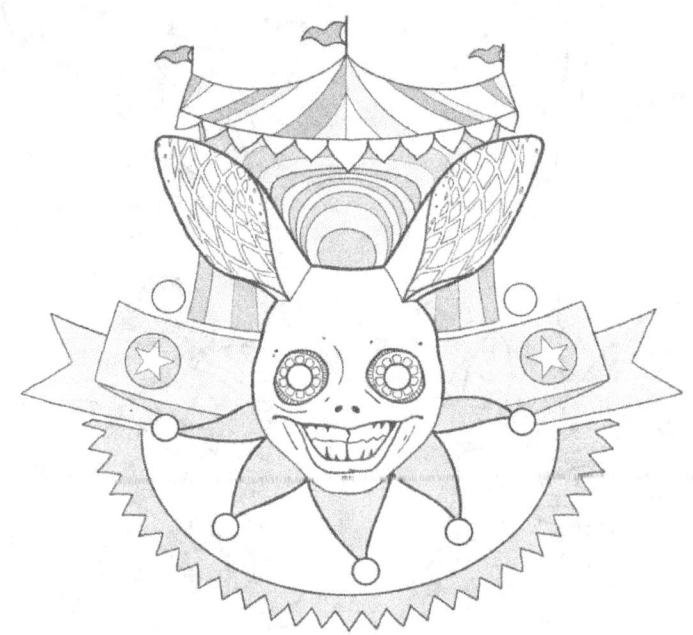

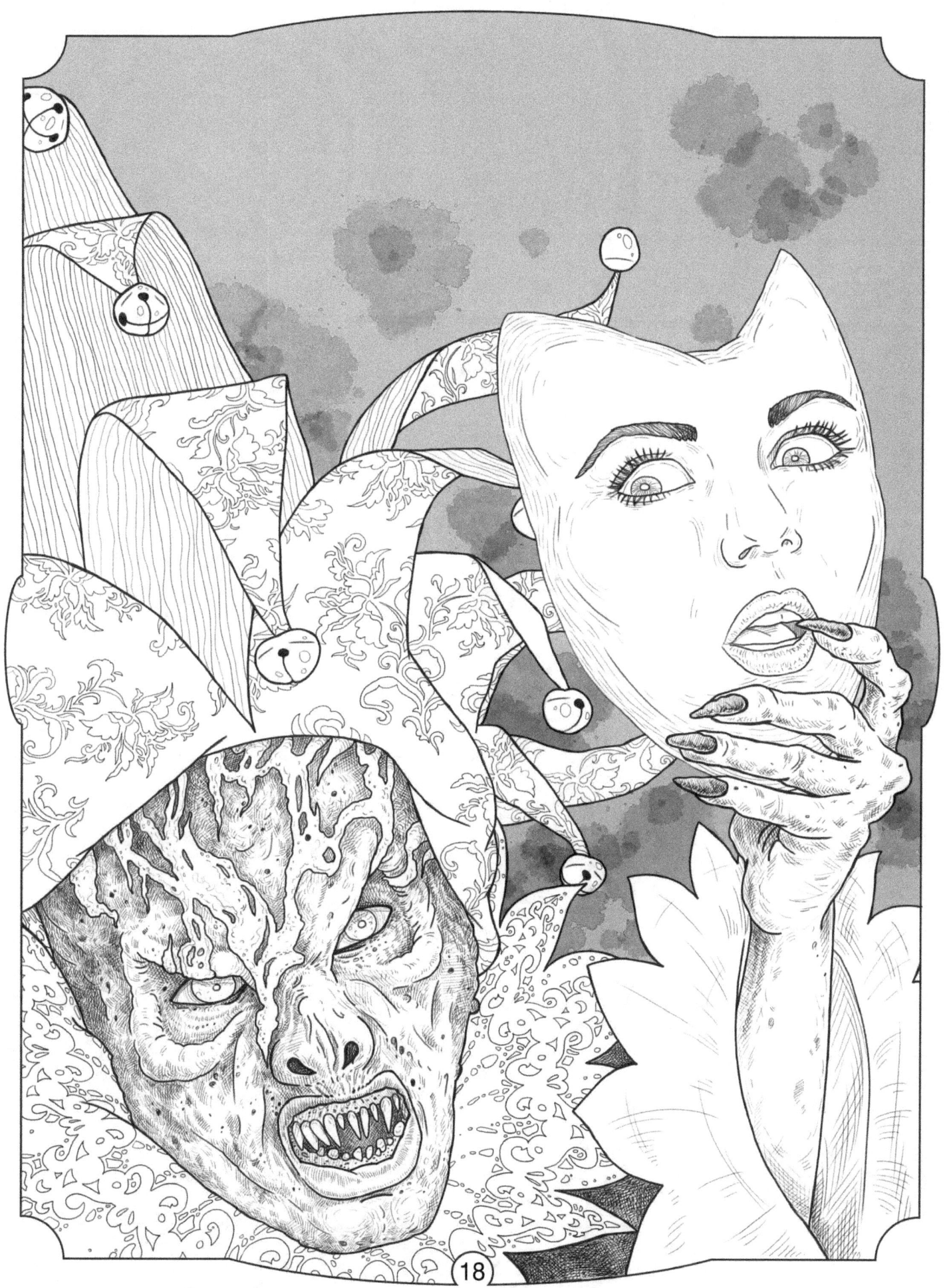

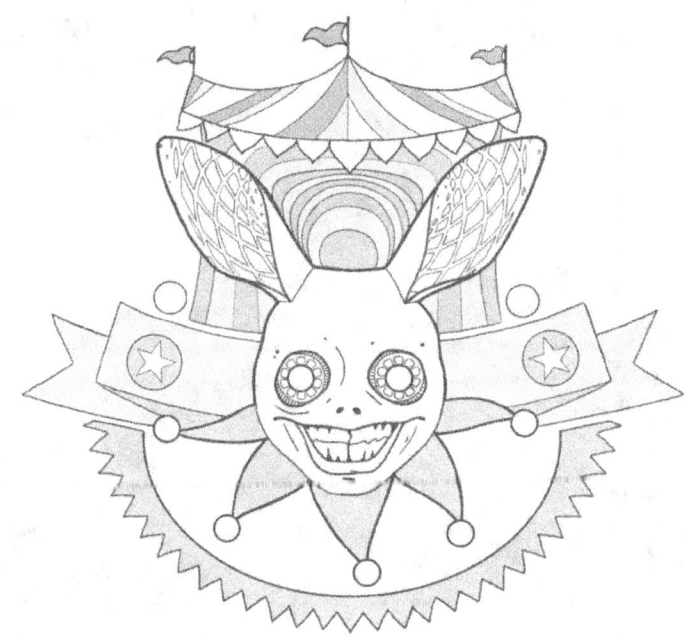

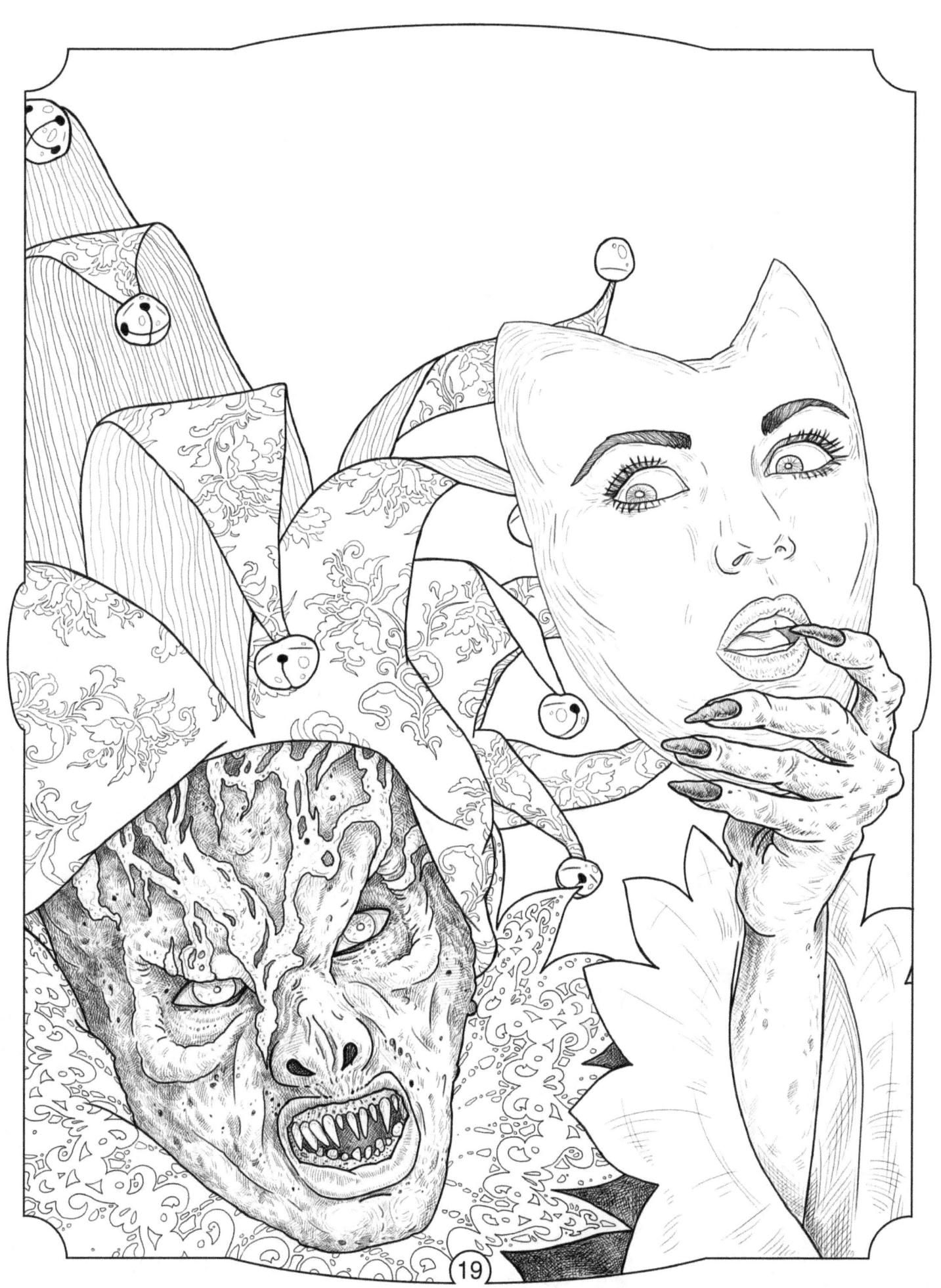

19

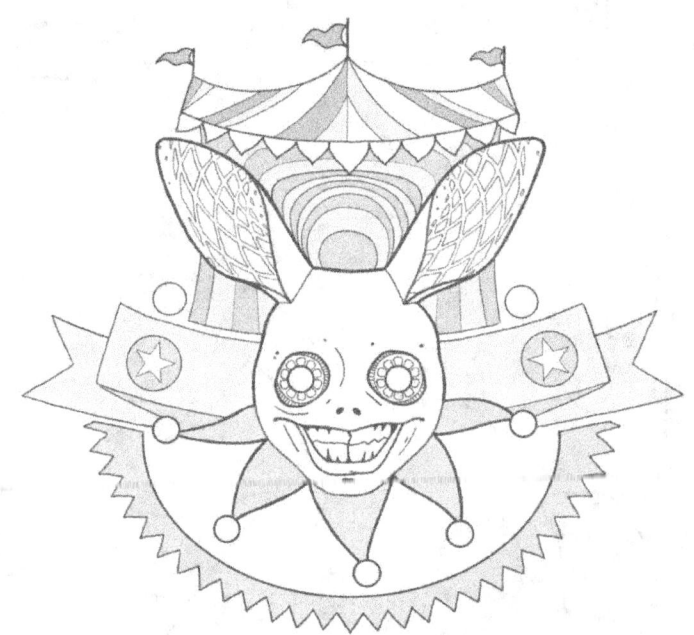

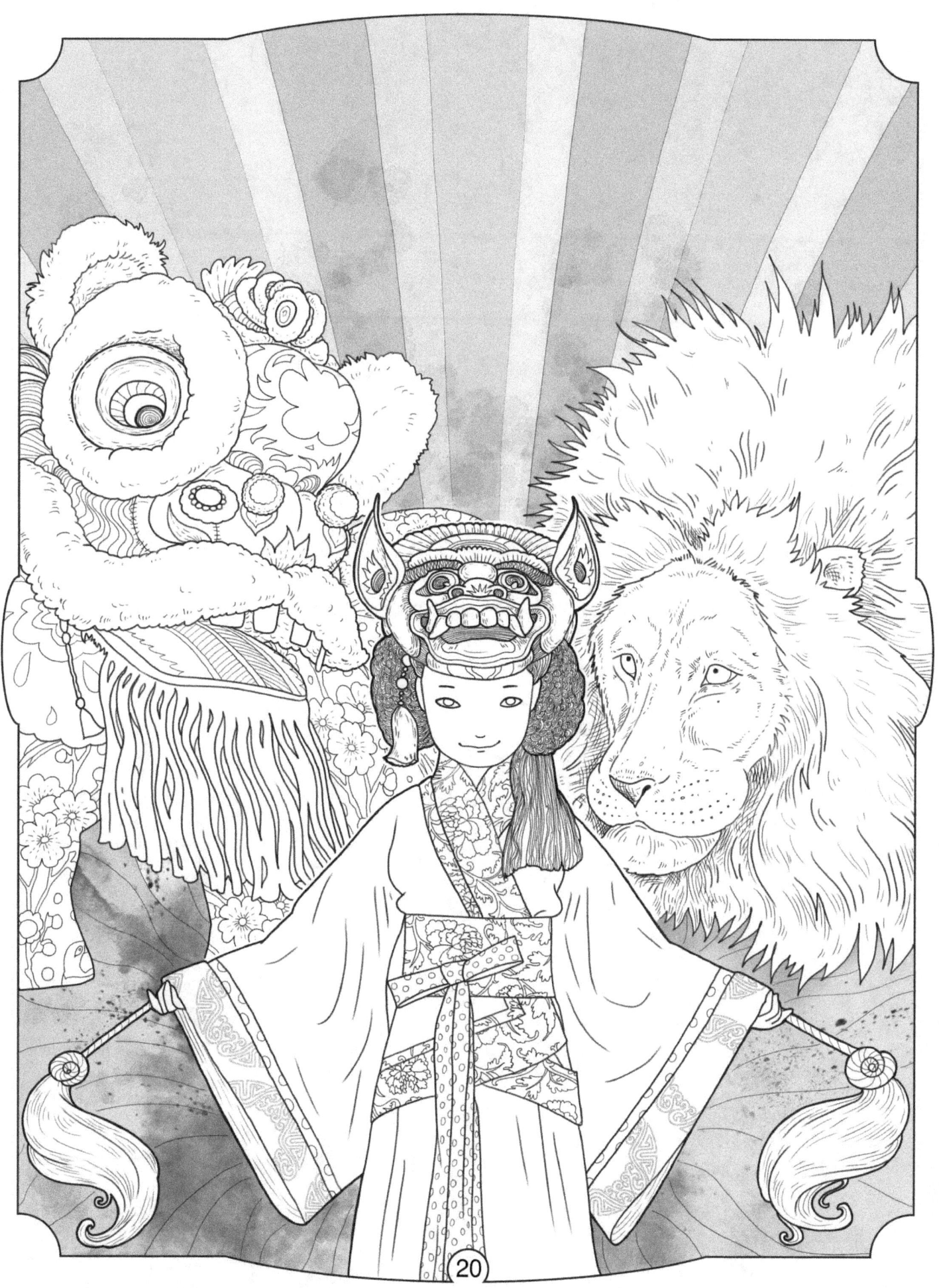

20

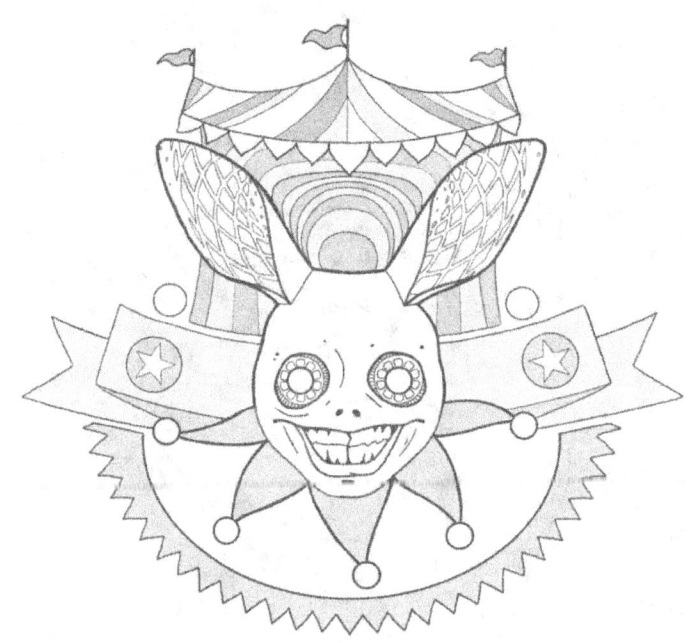

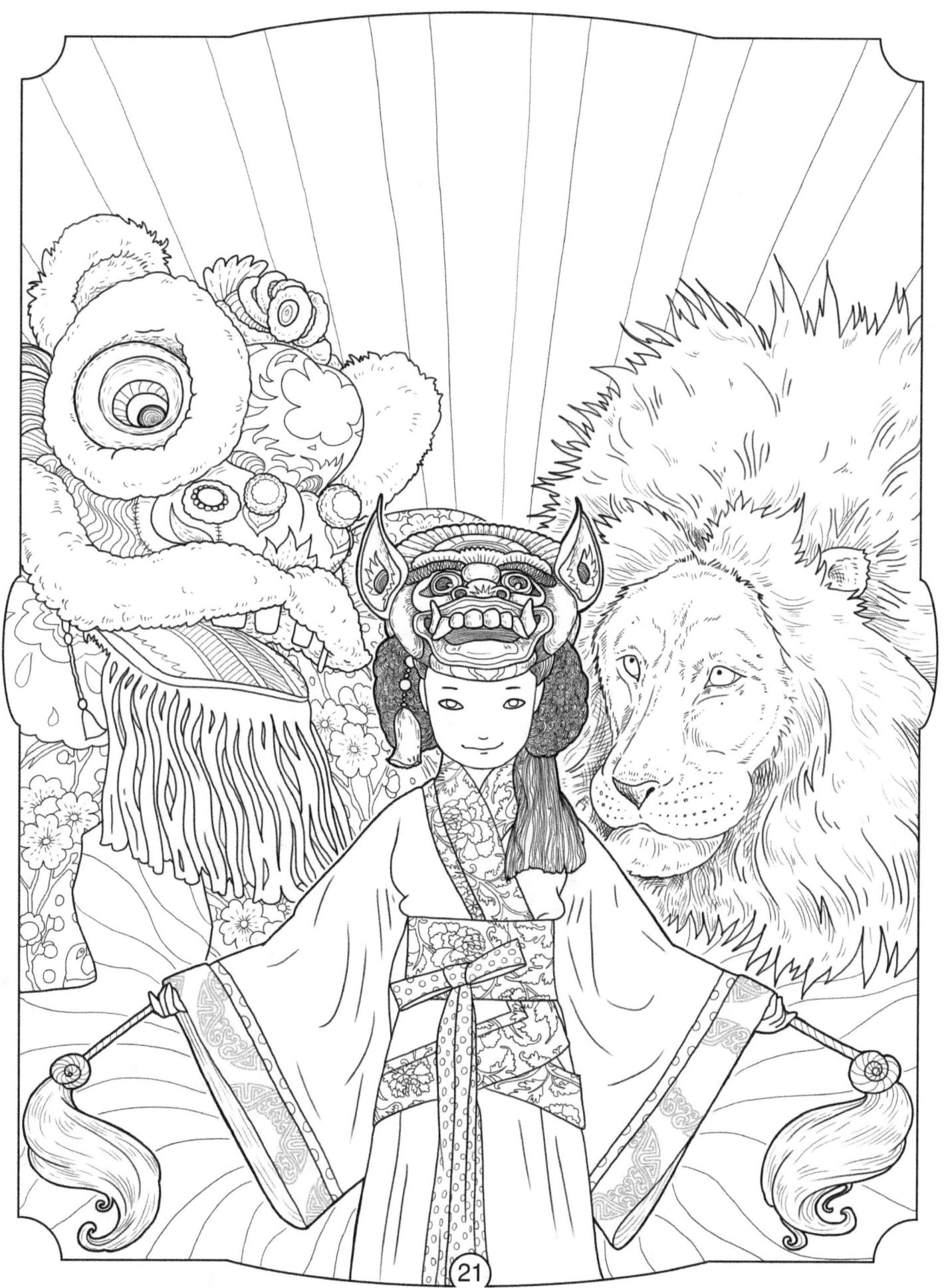

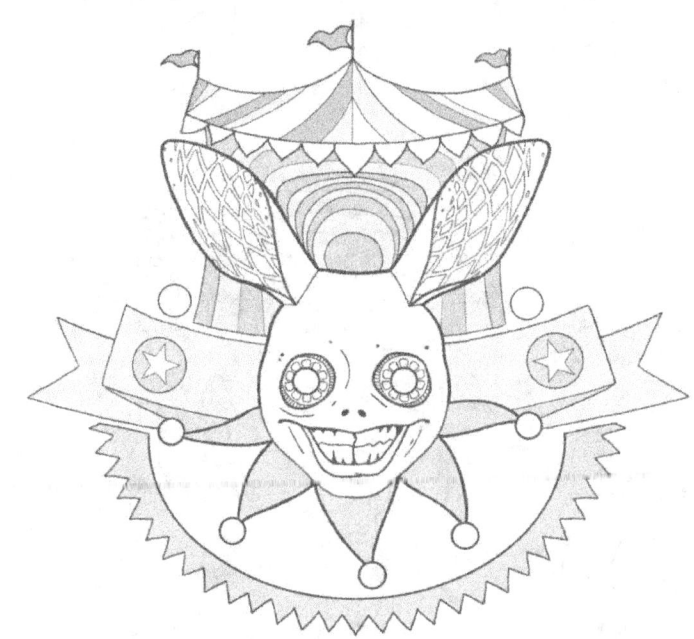

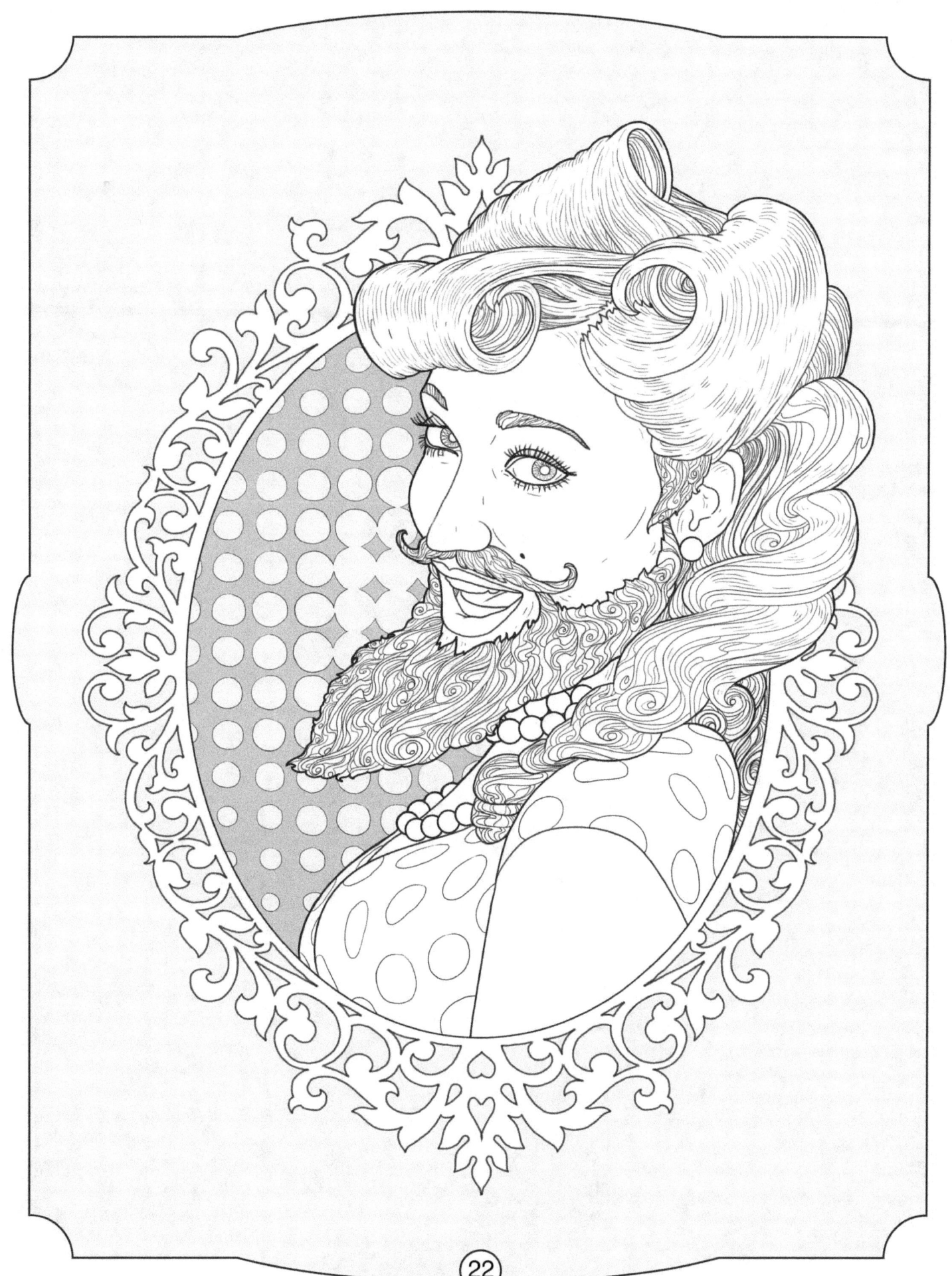

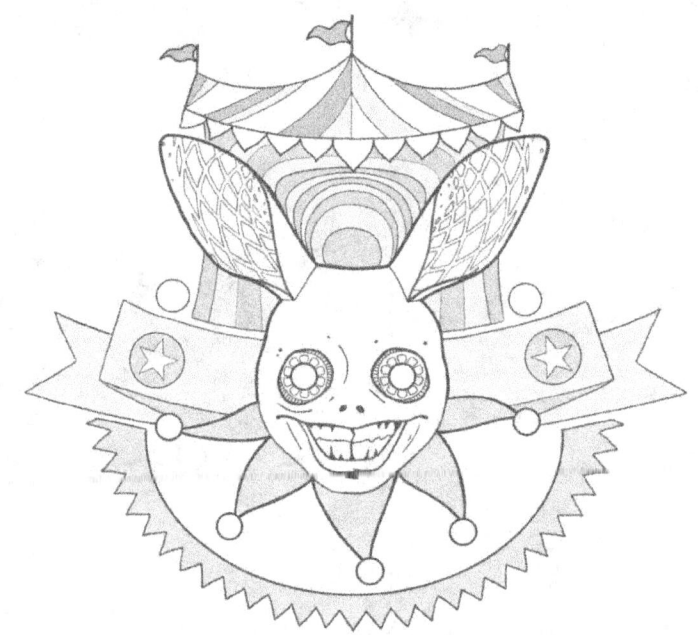

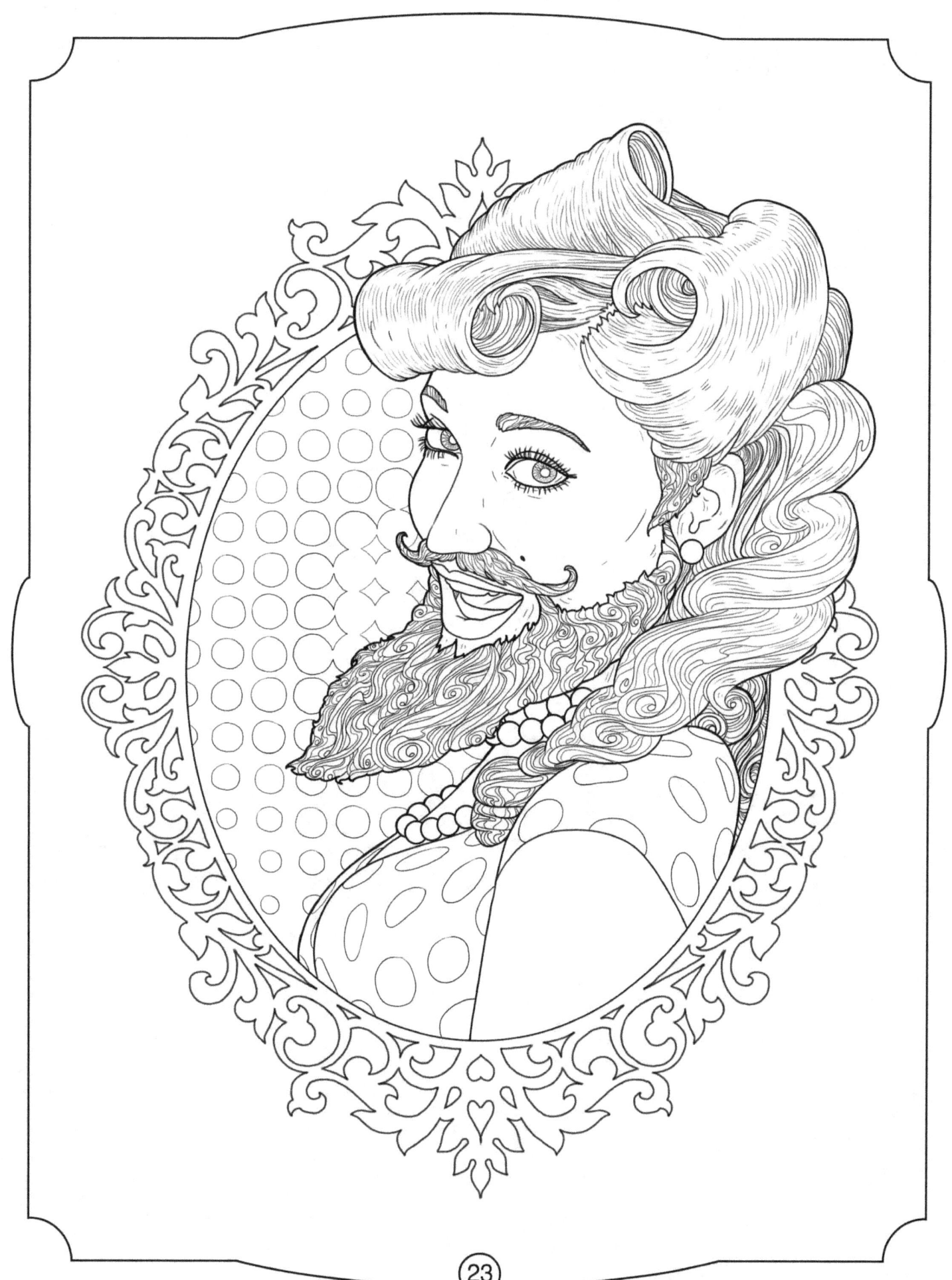

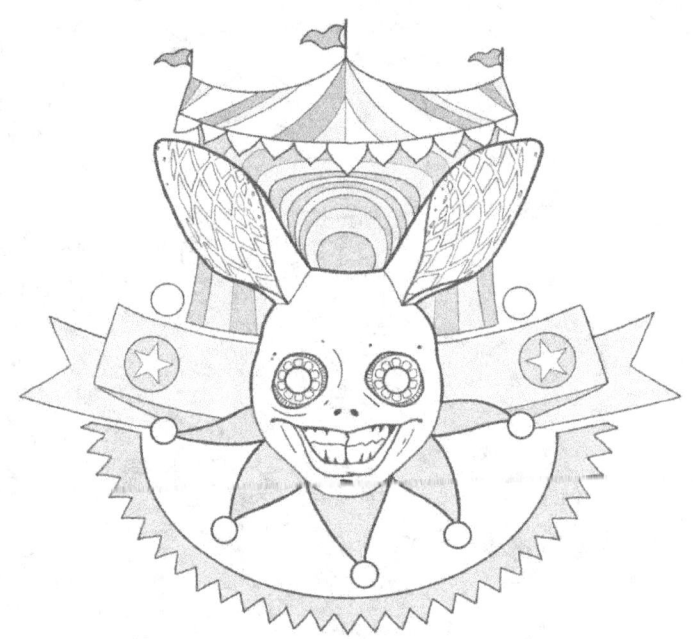

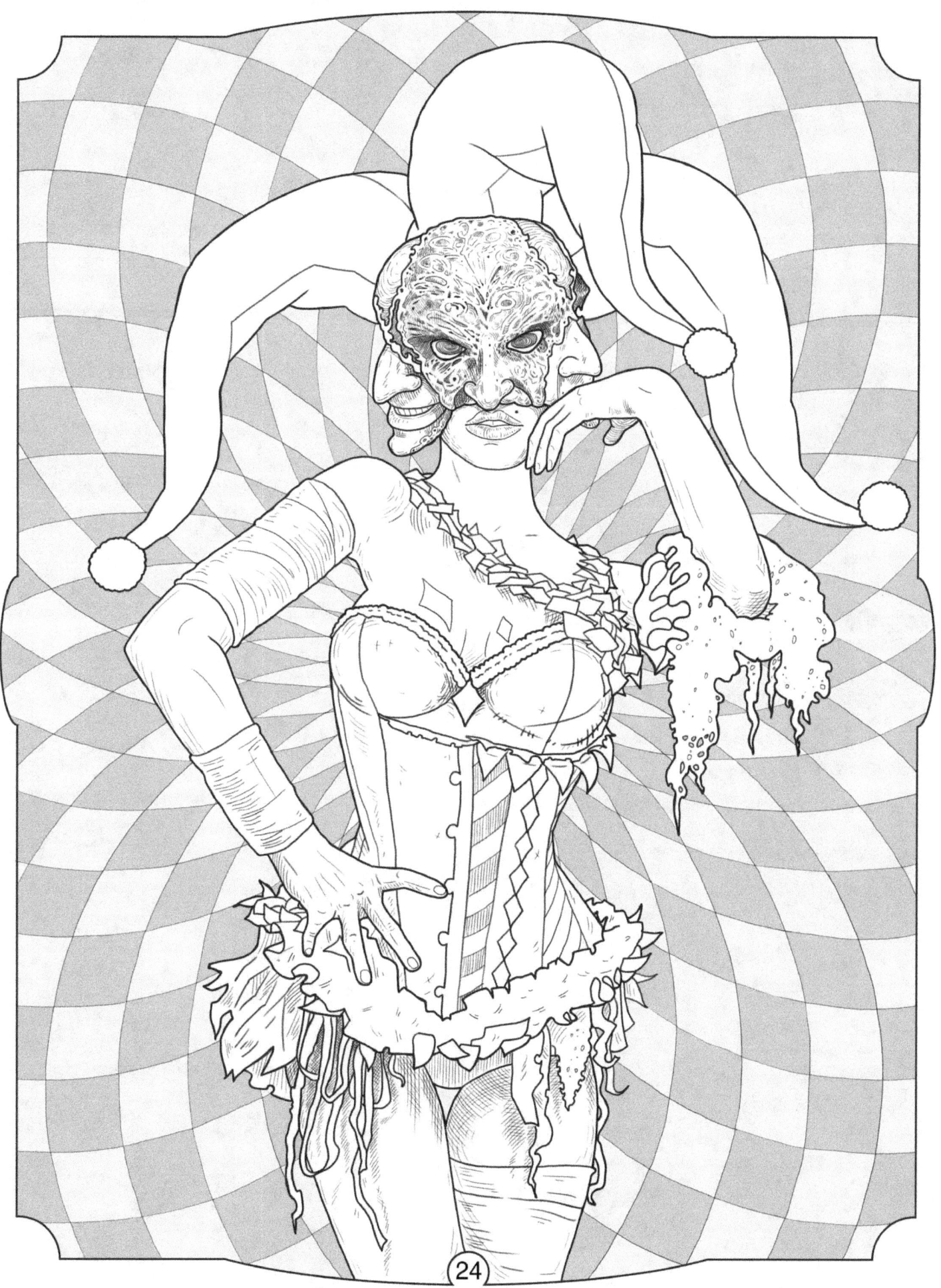

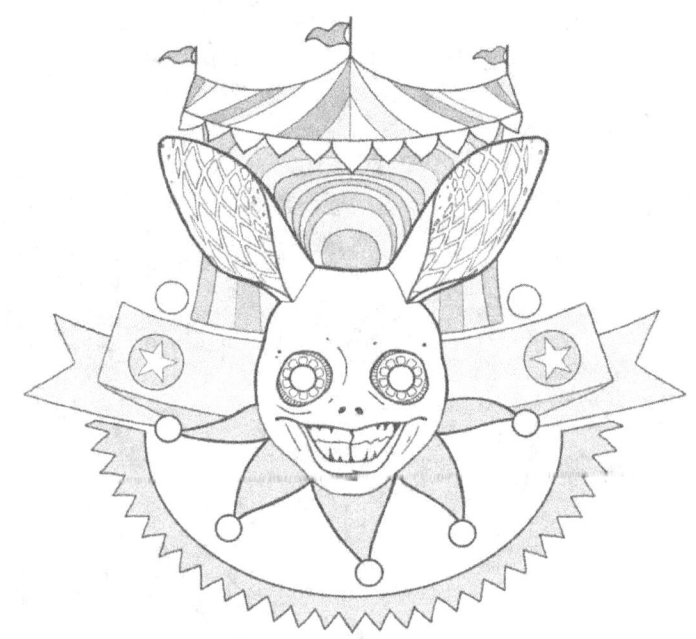

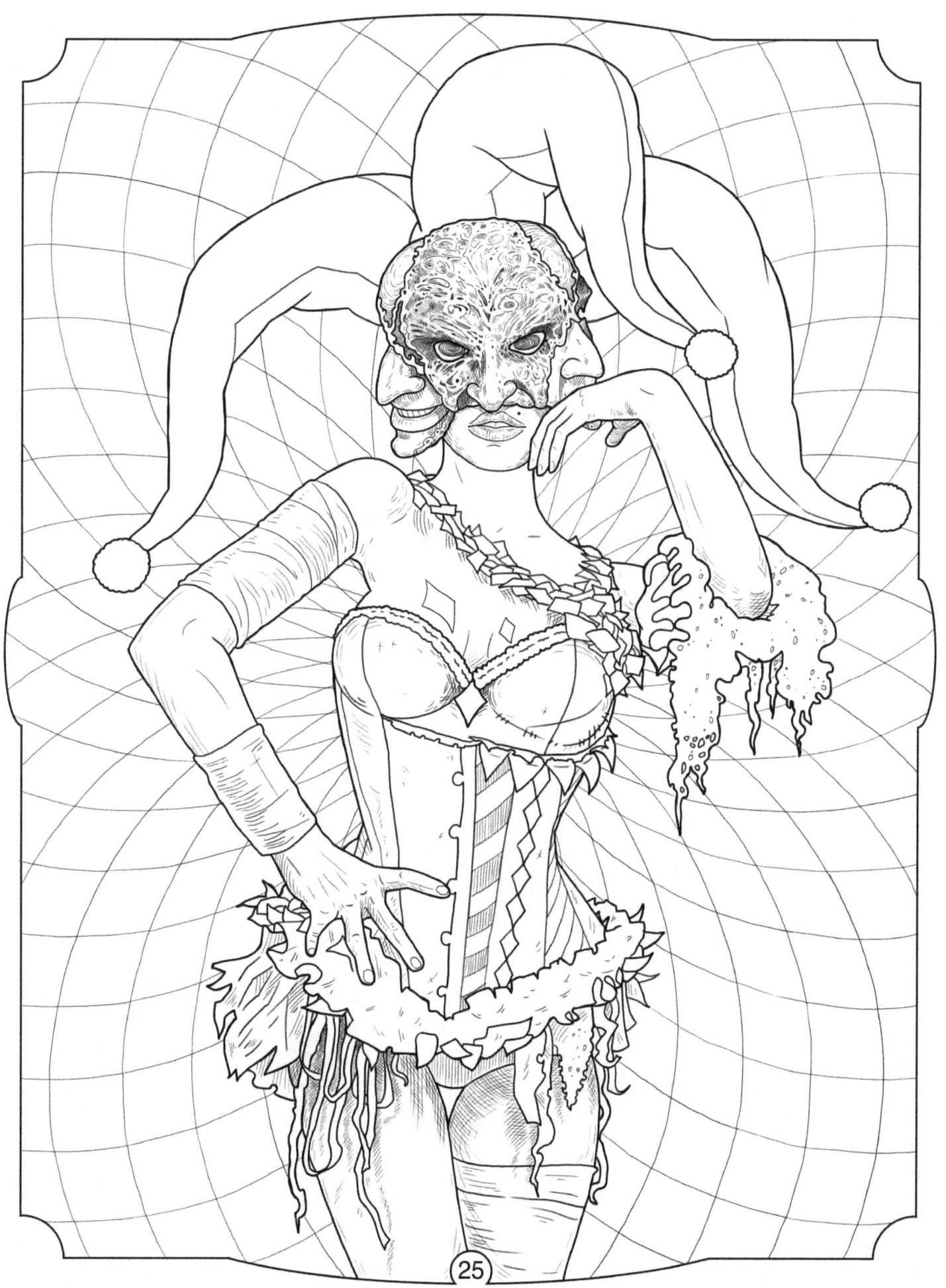

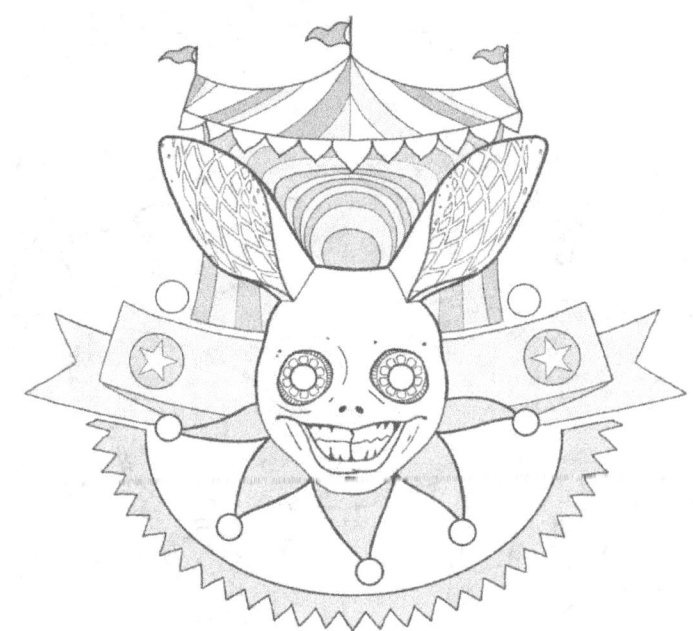

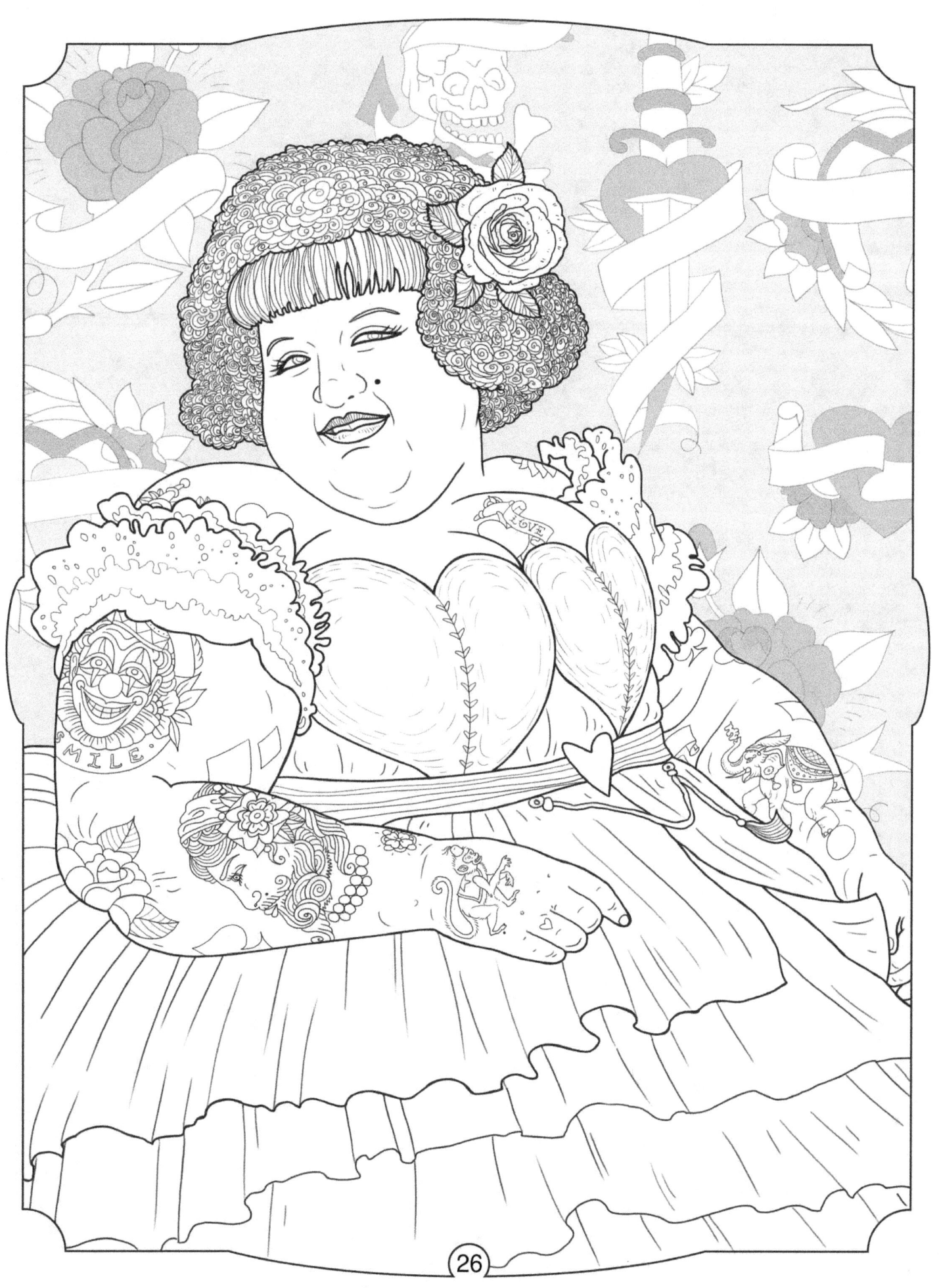

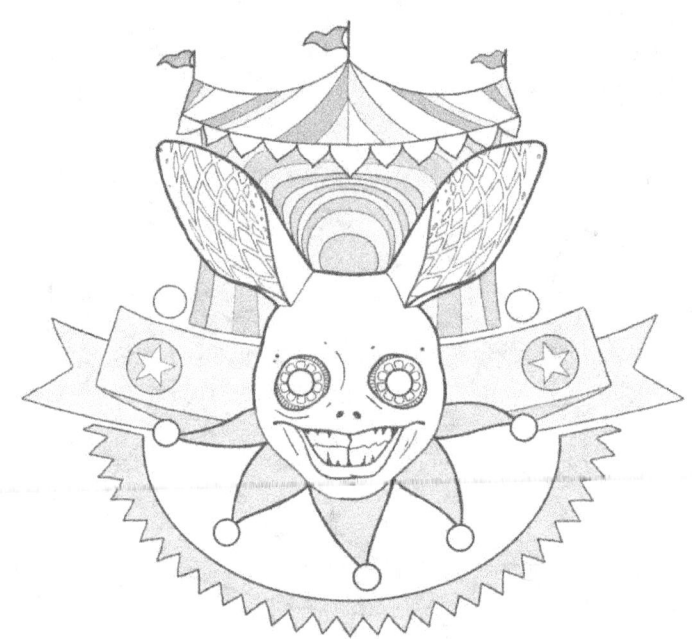

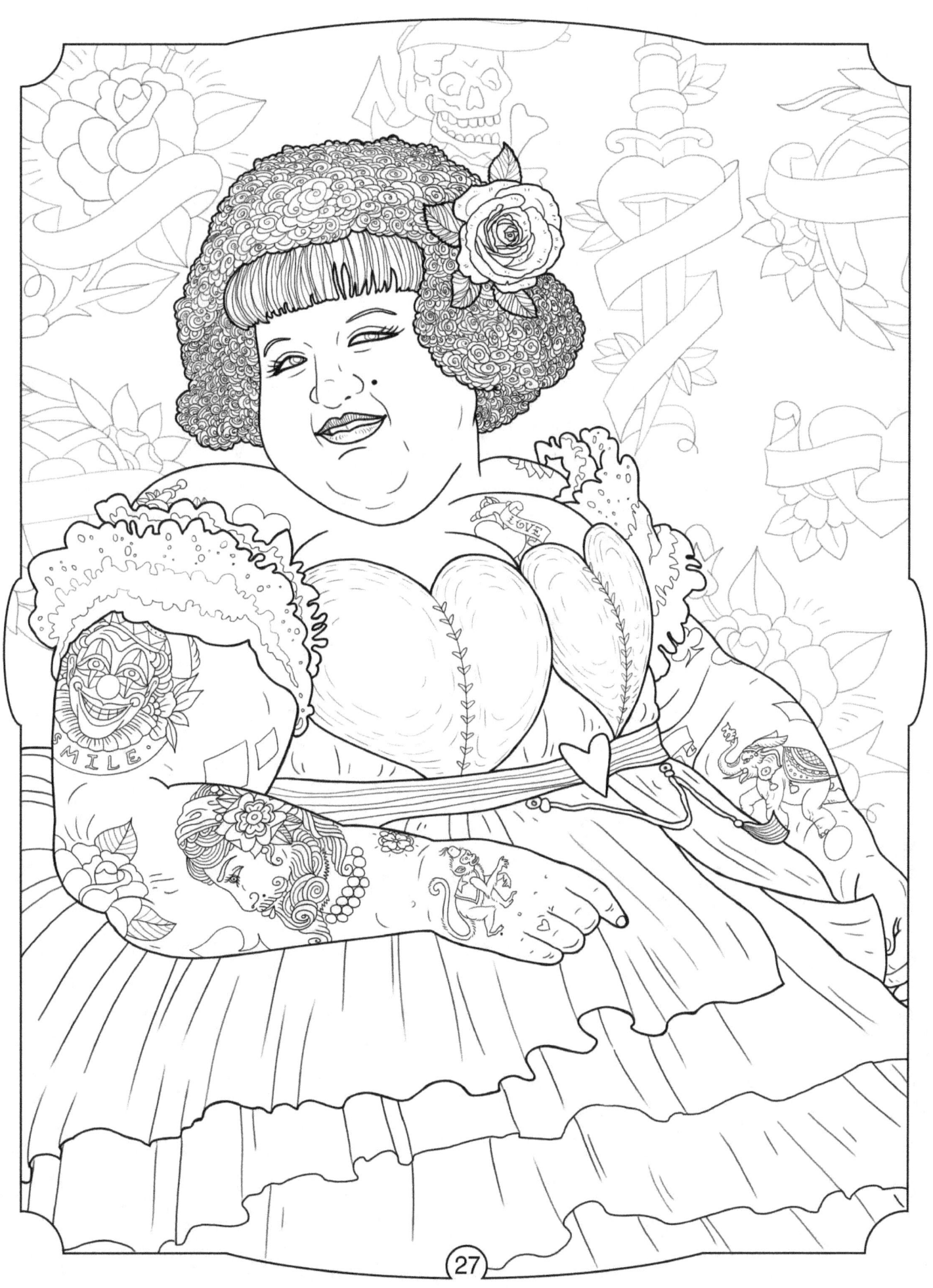

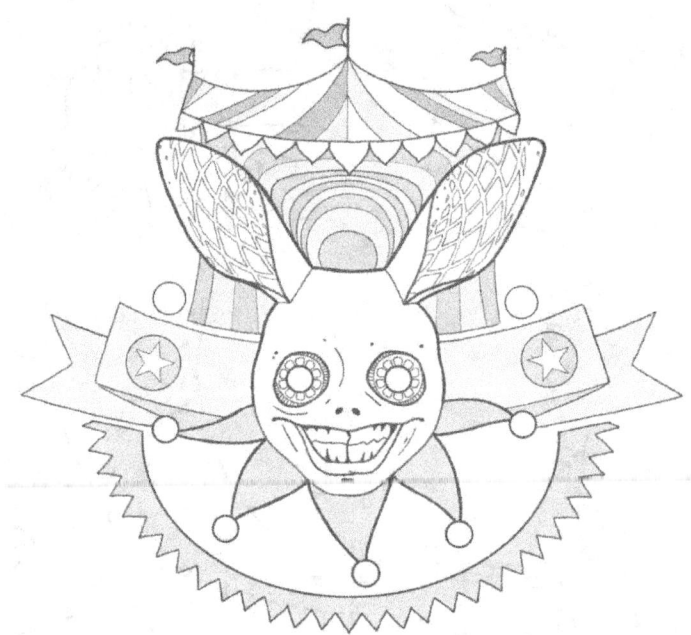

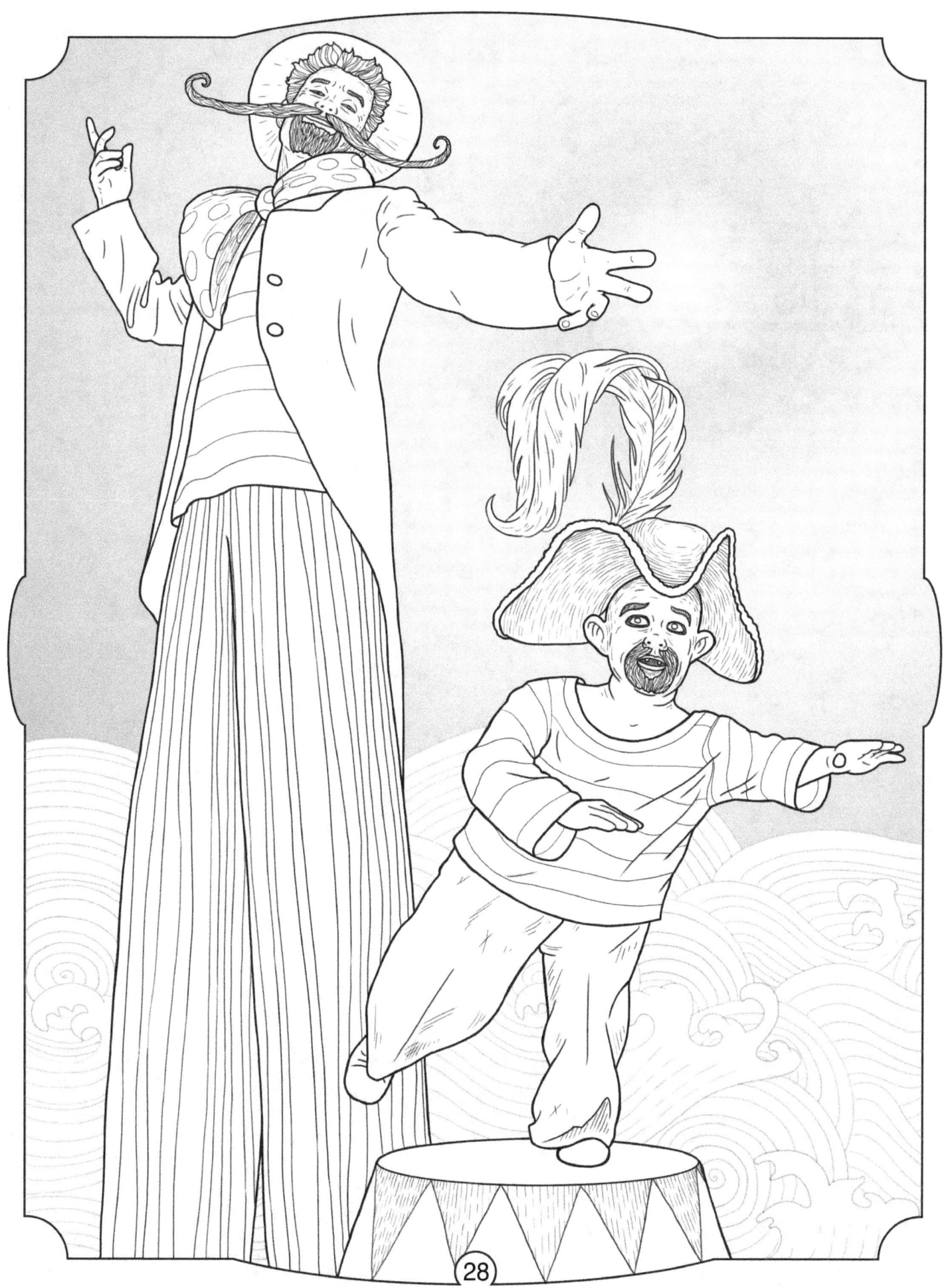

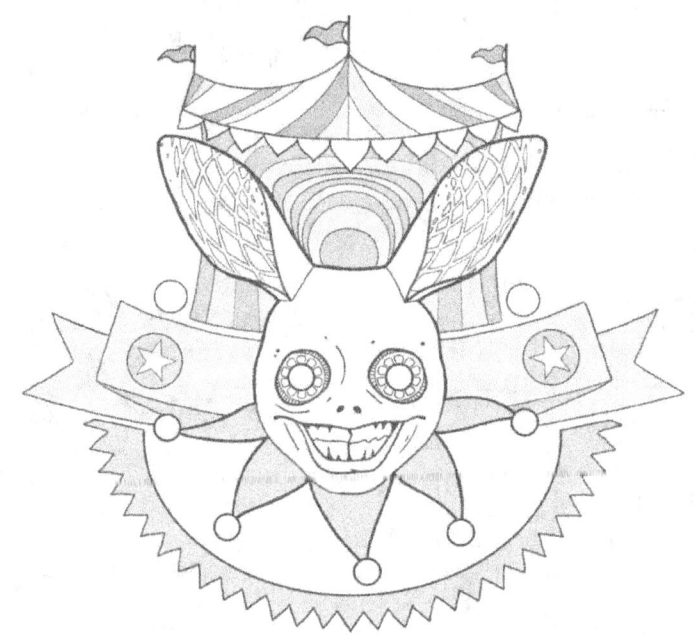

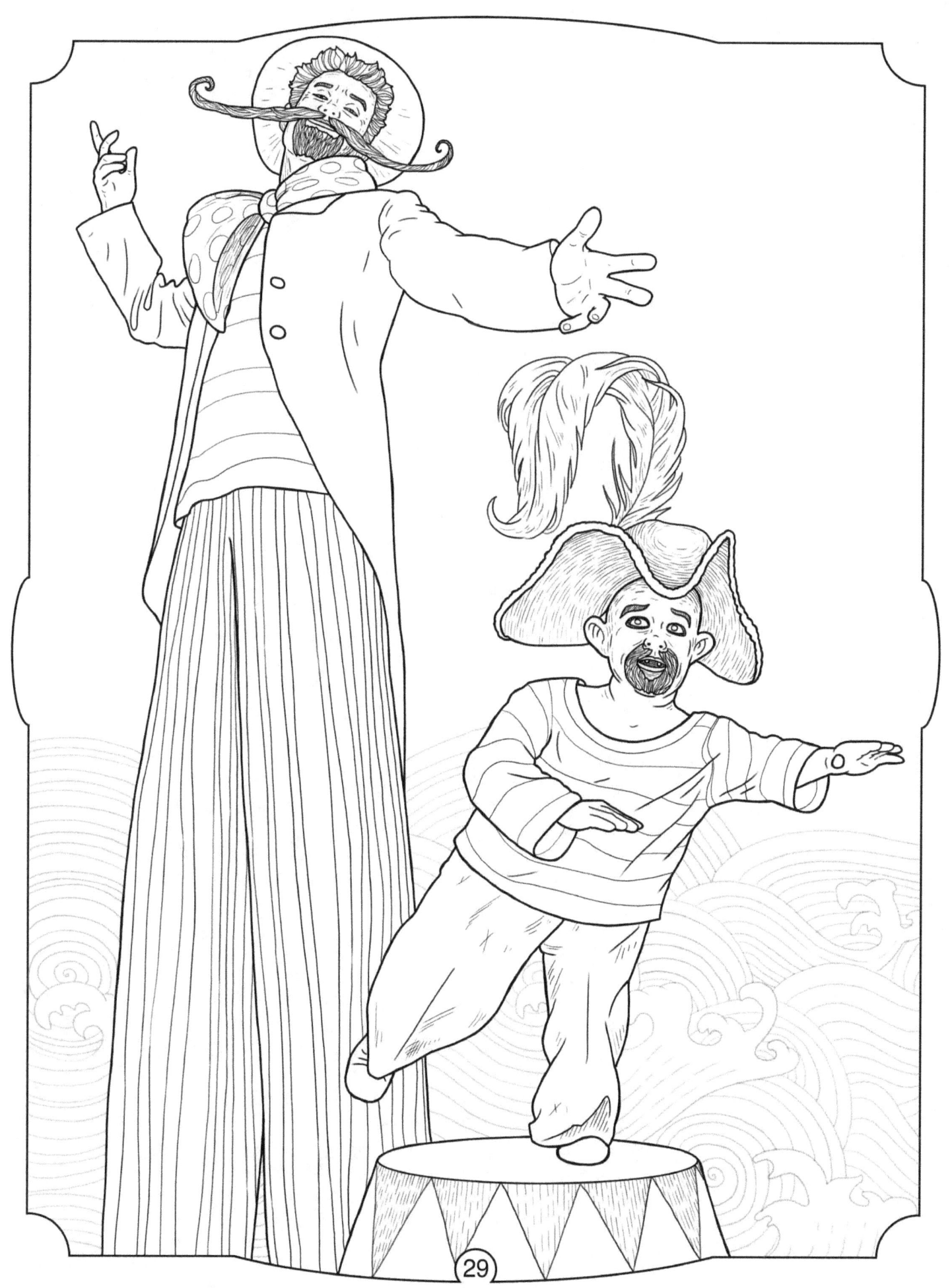

29

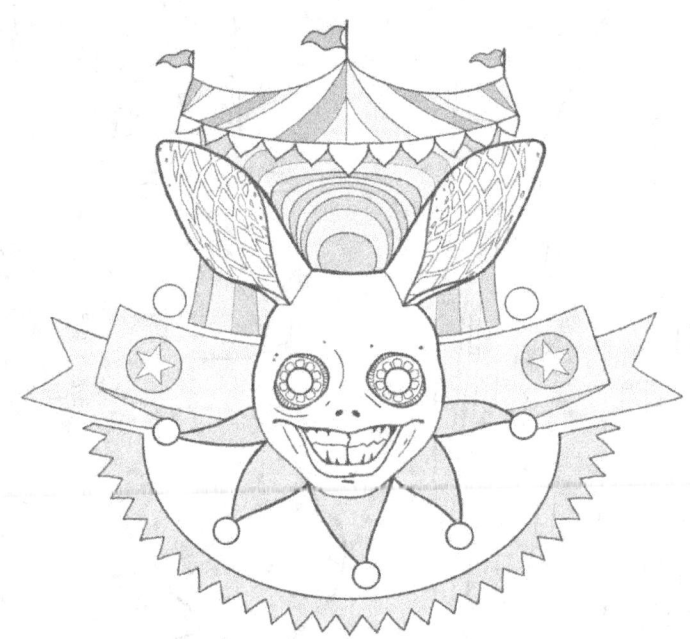

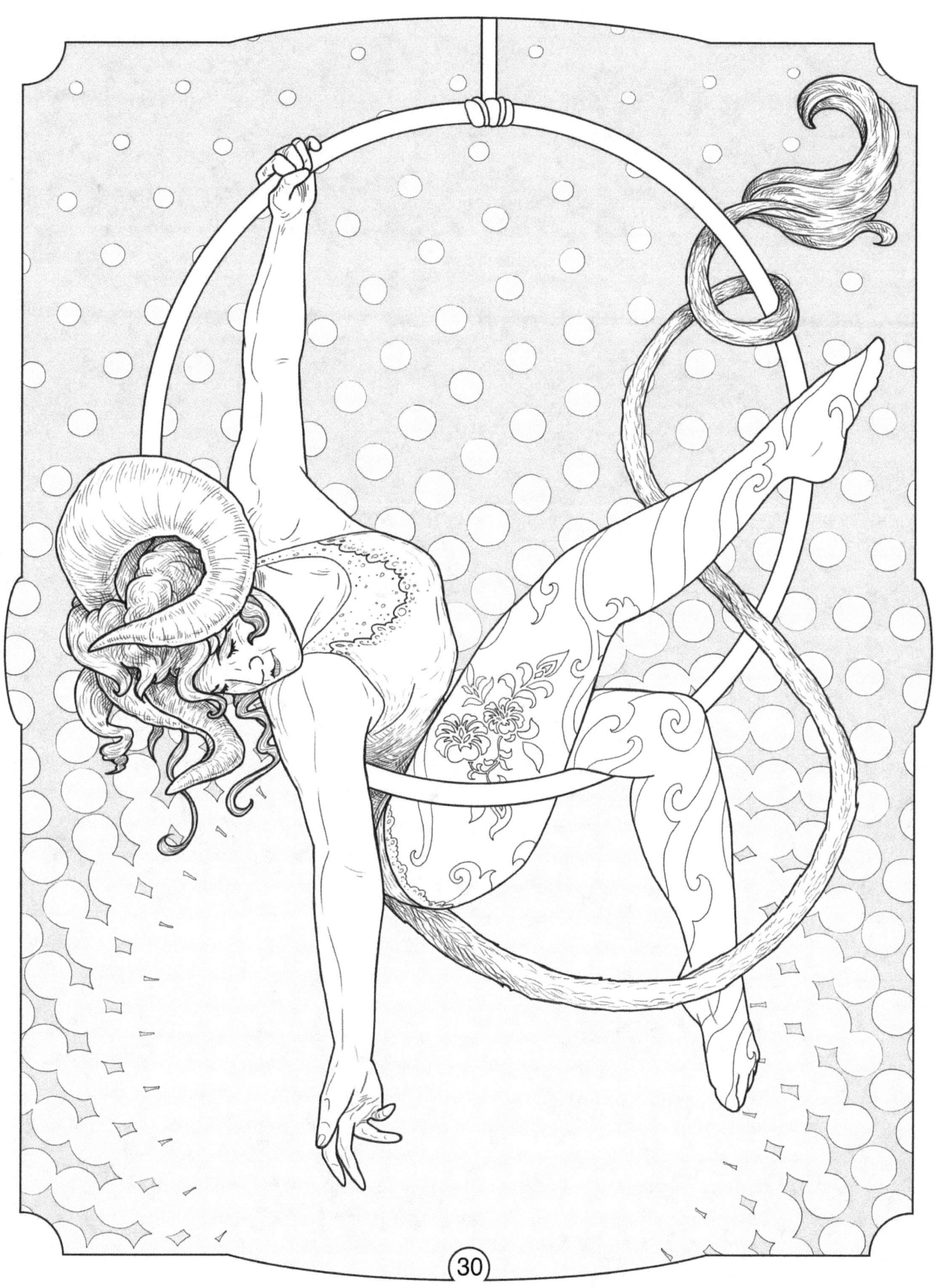

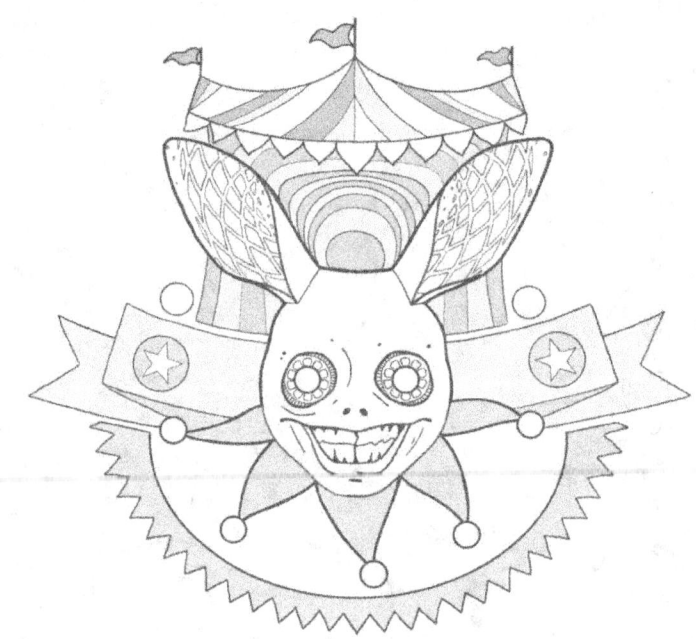

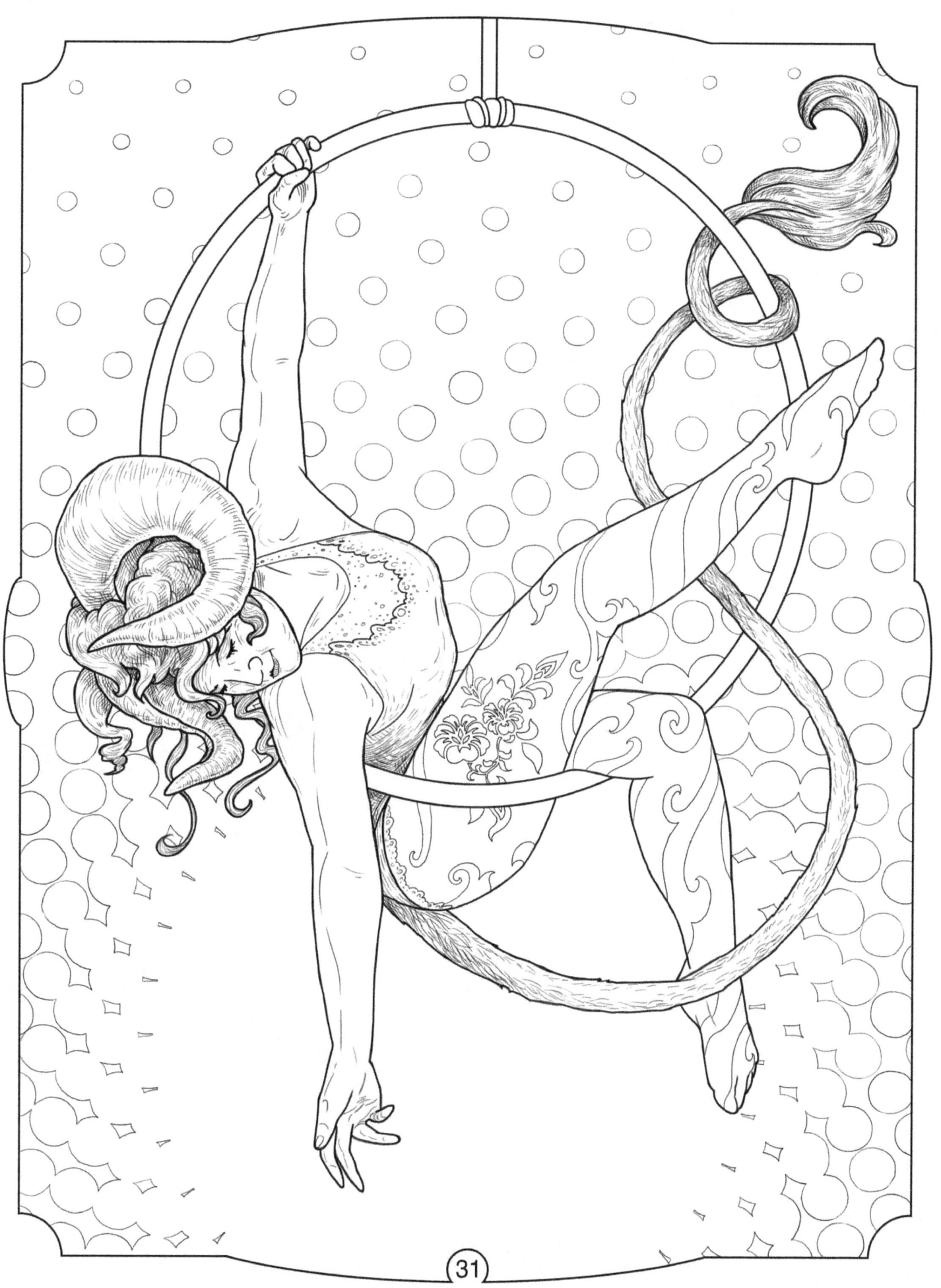

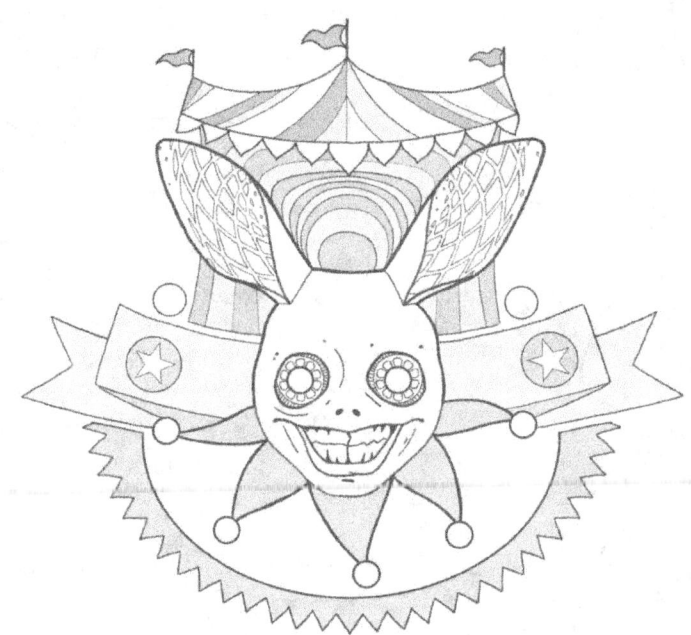

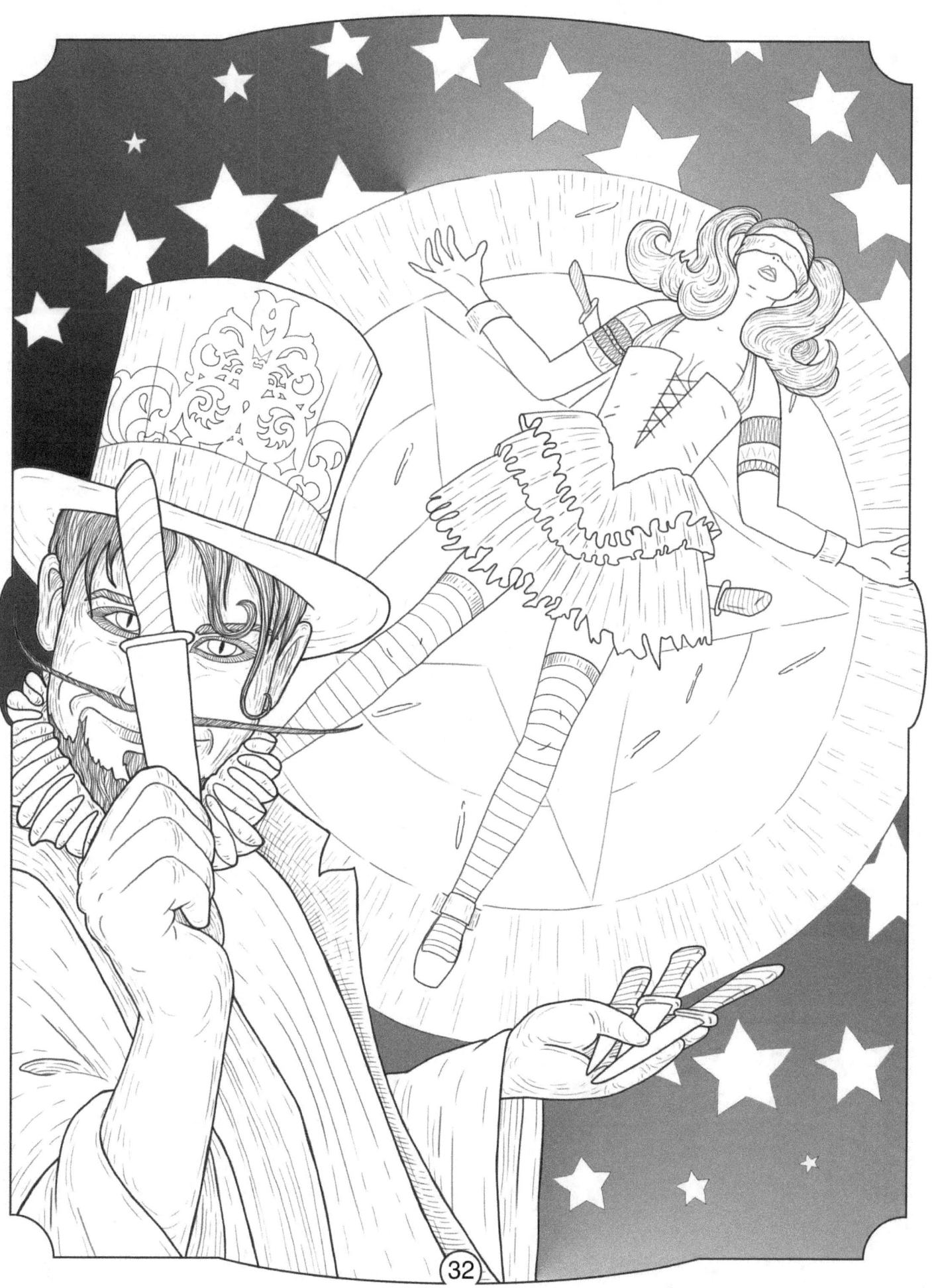

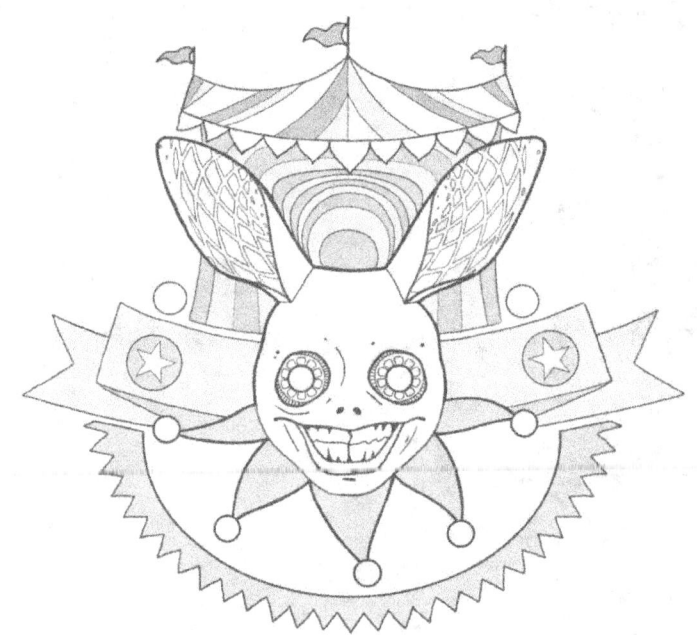

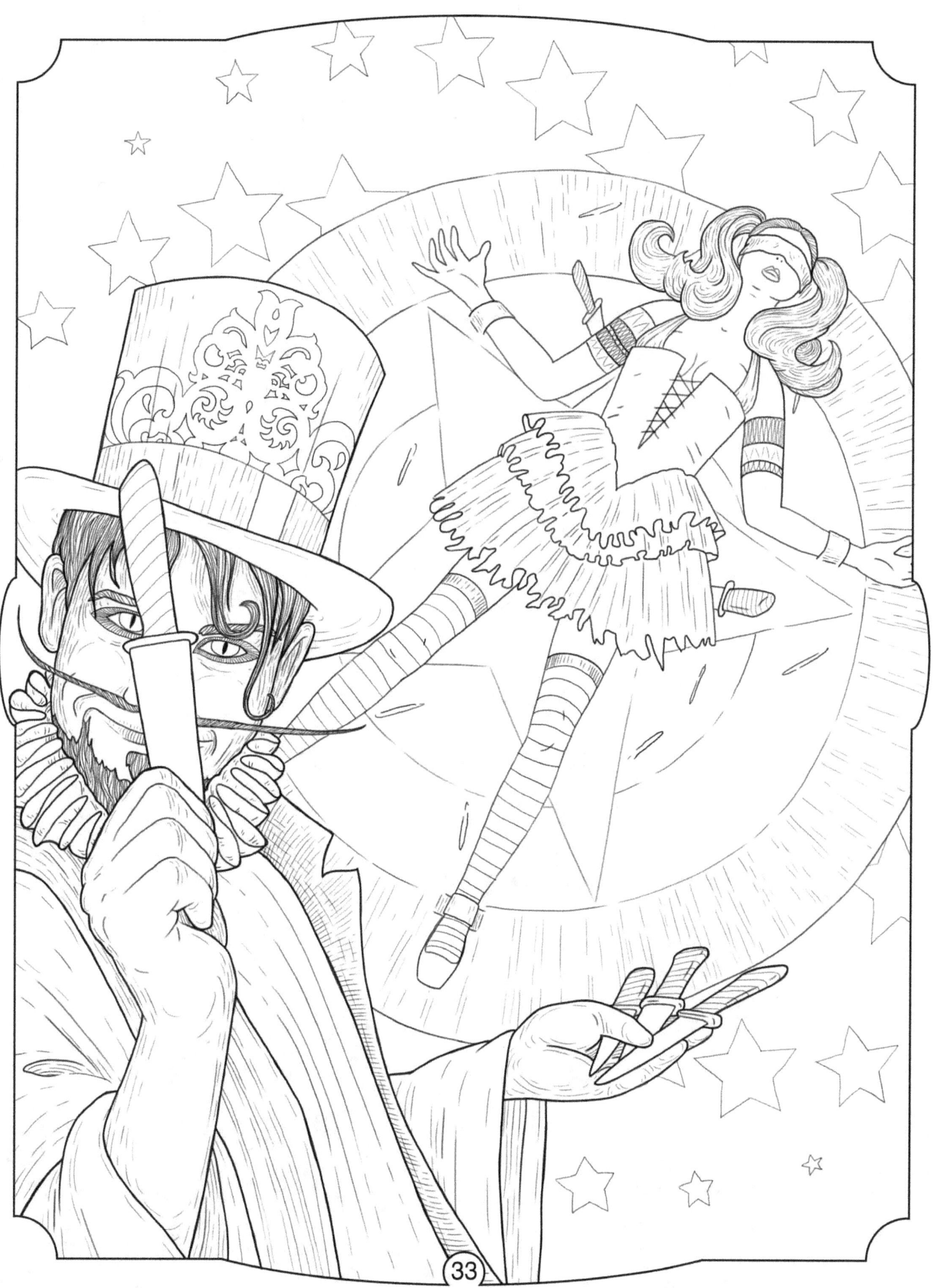

33

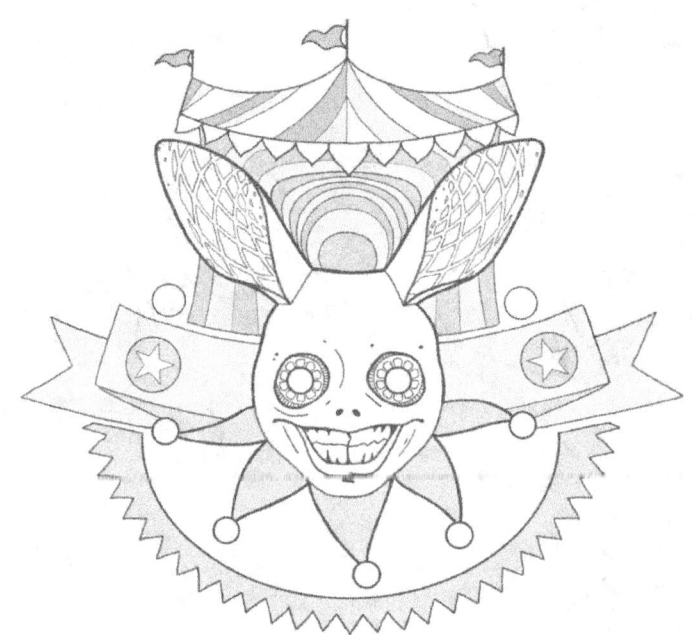

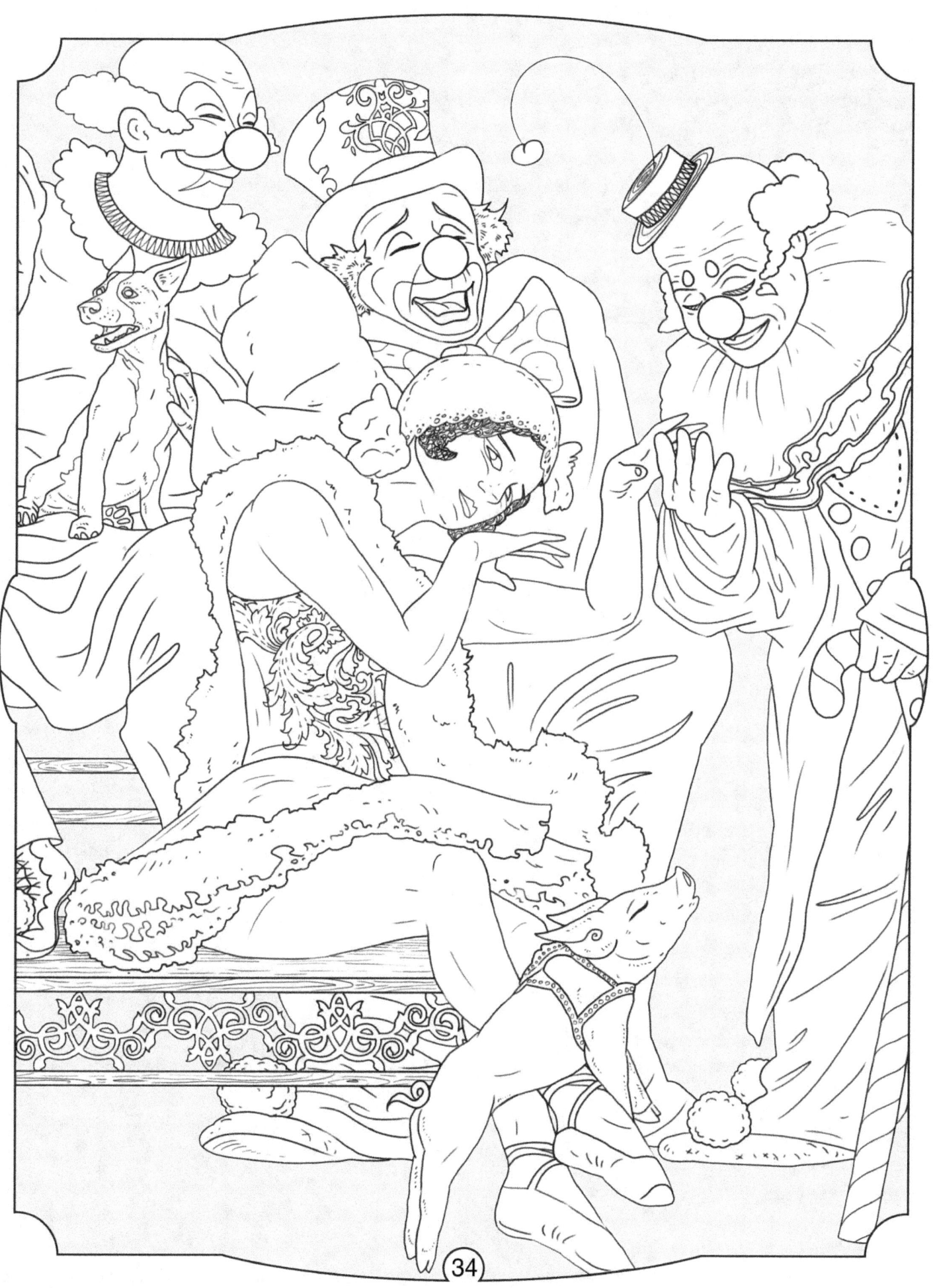

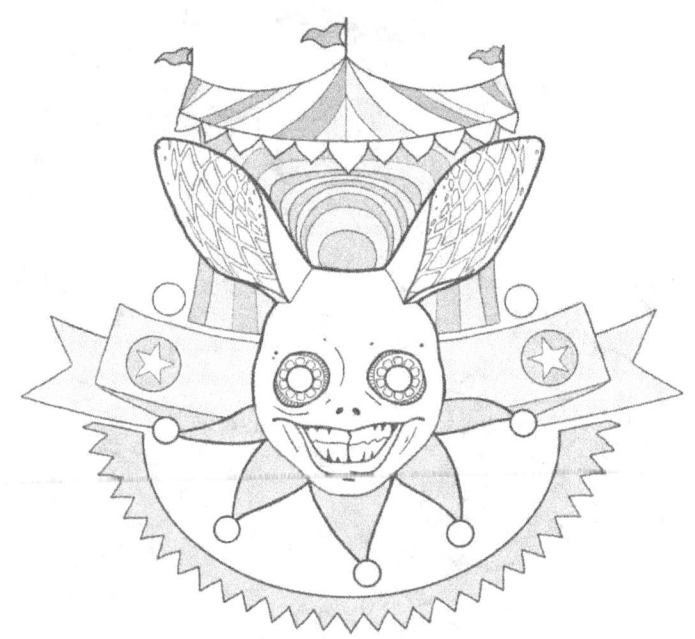

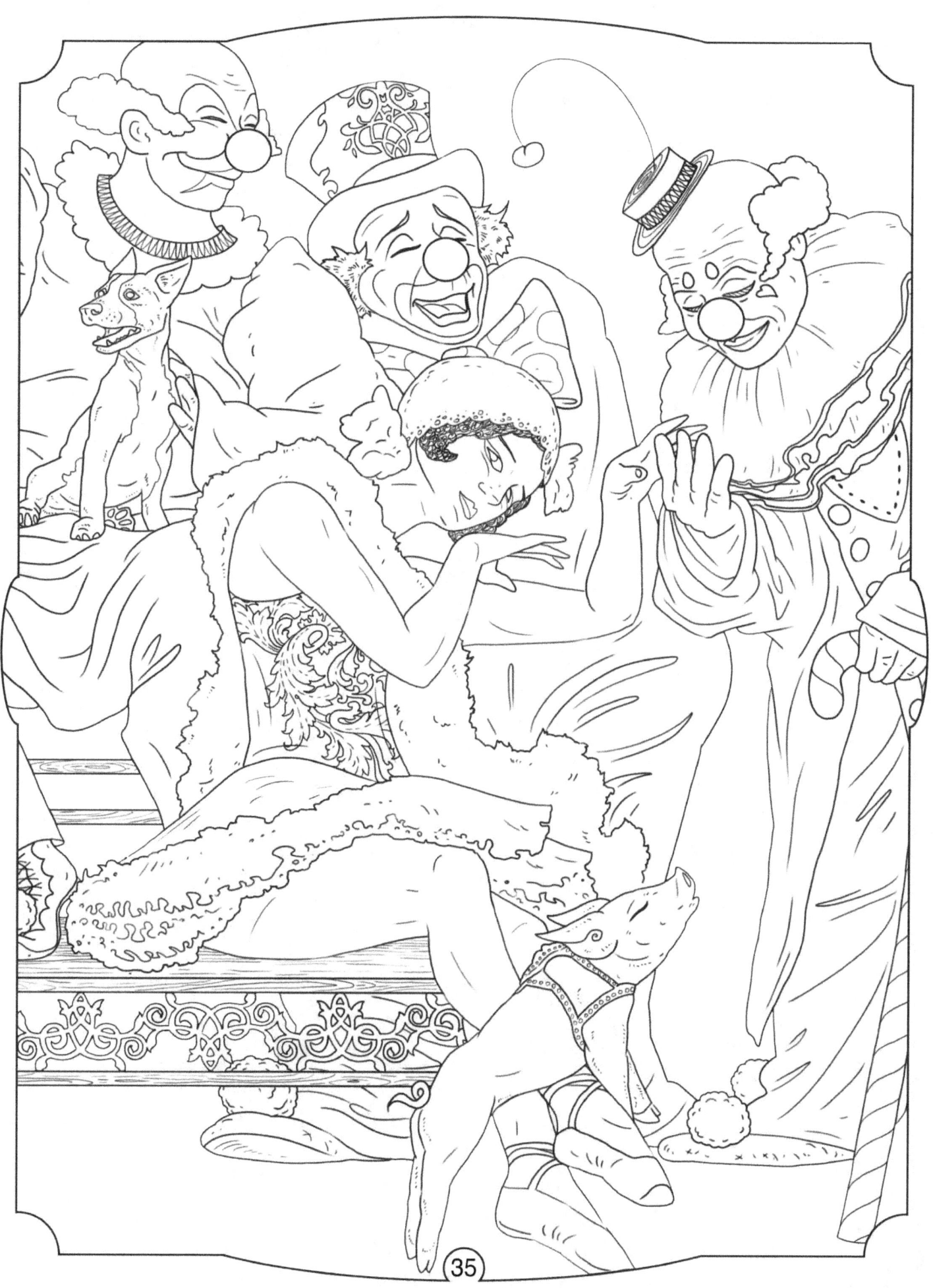

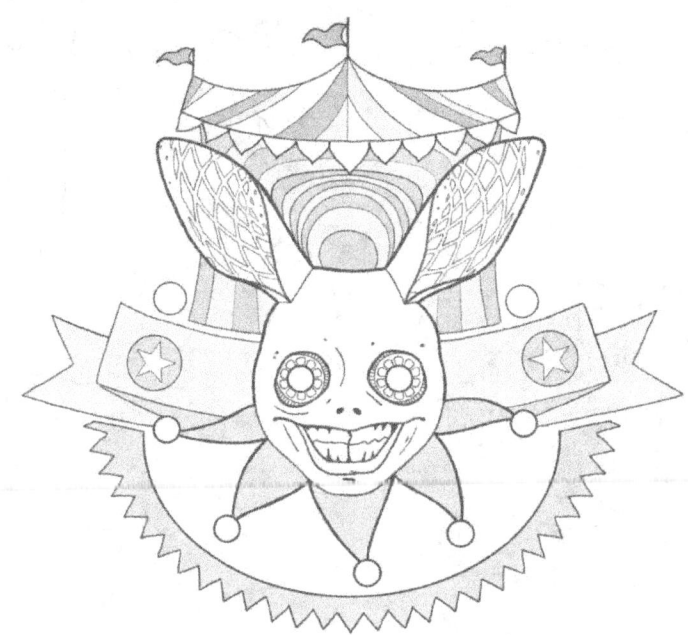

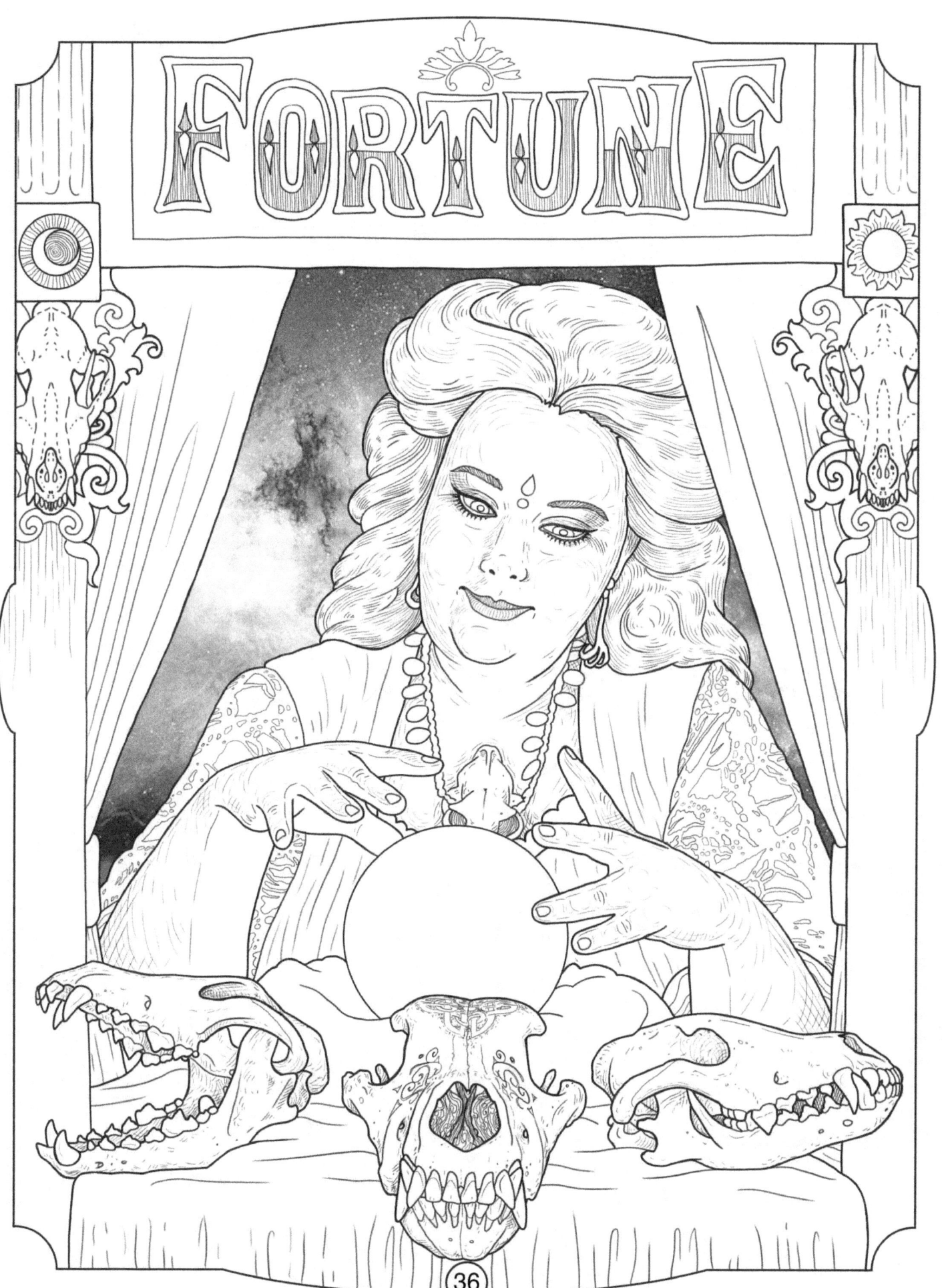

FORTUNE

36

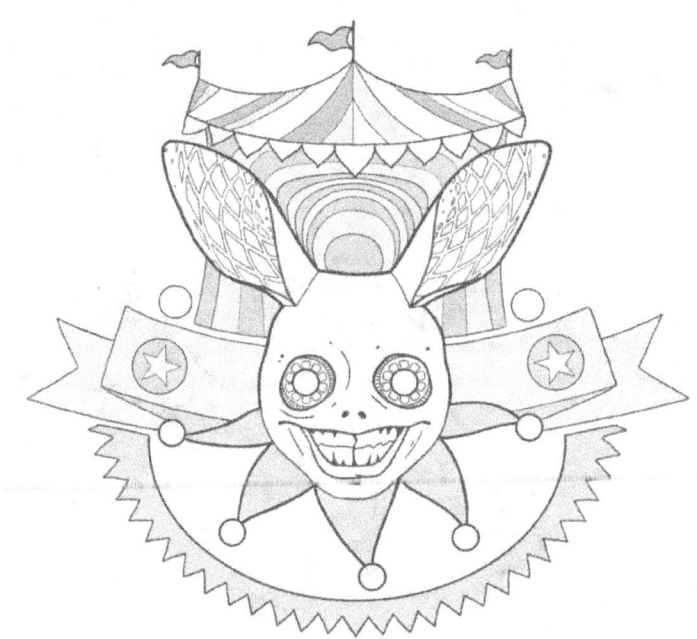

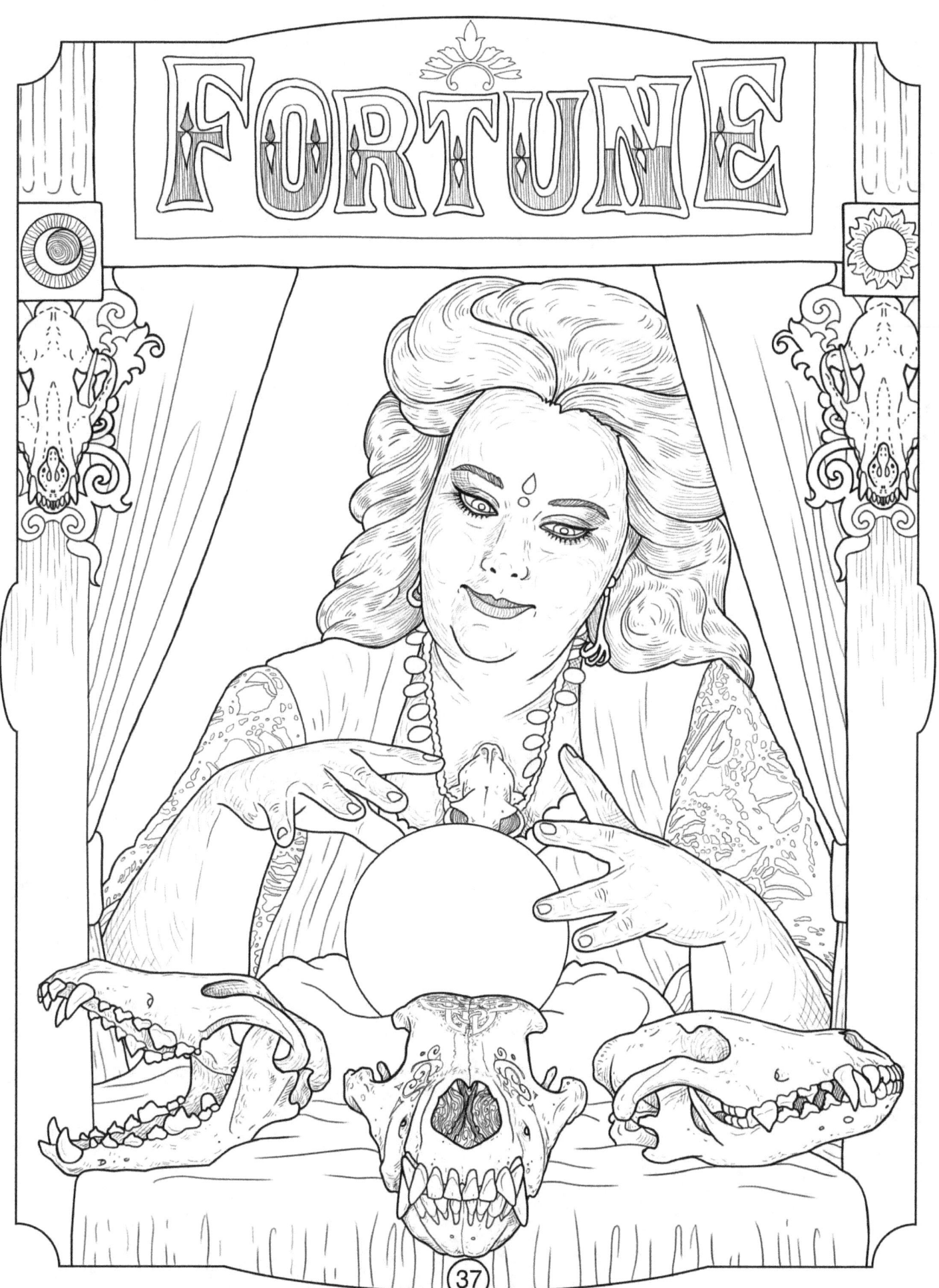

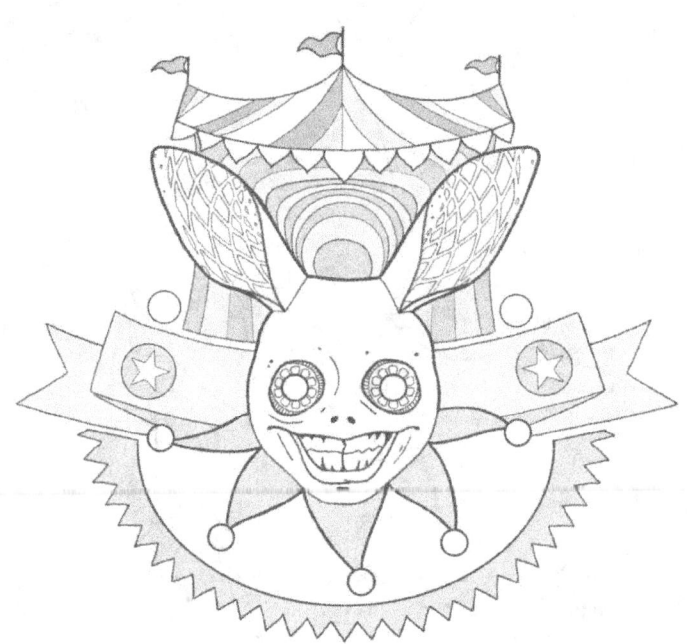

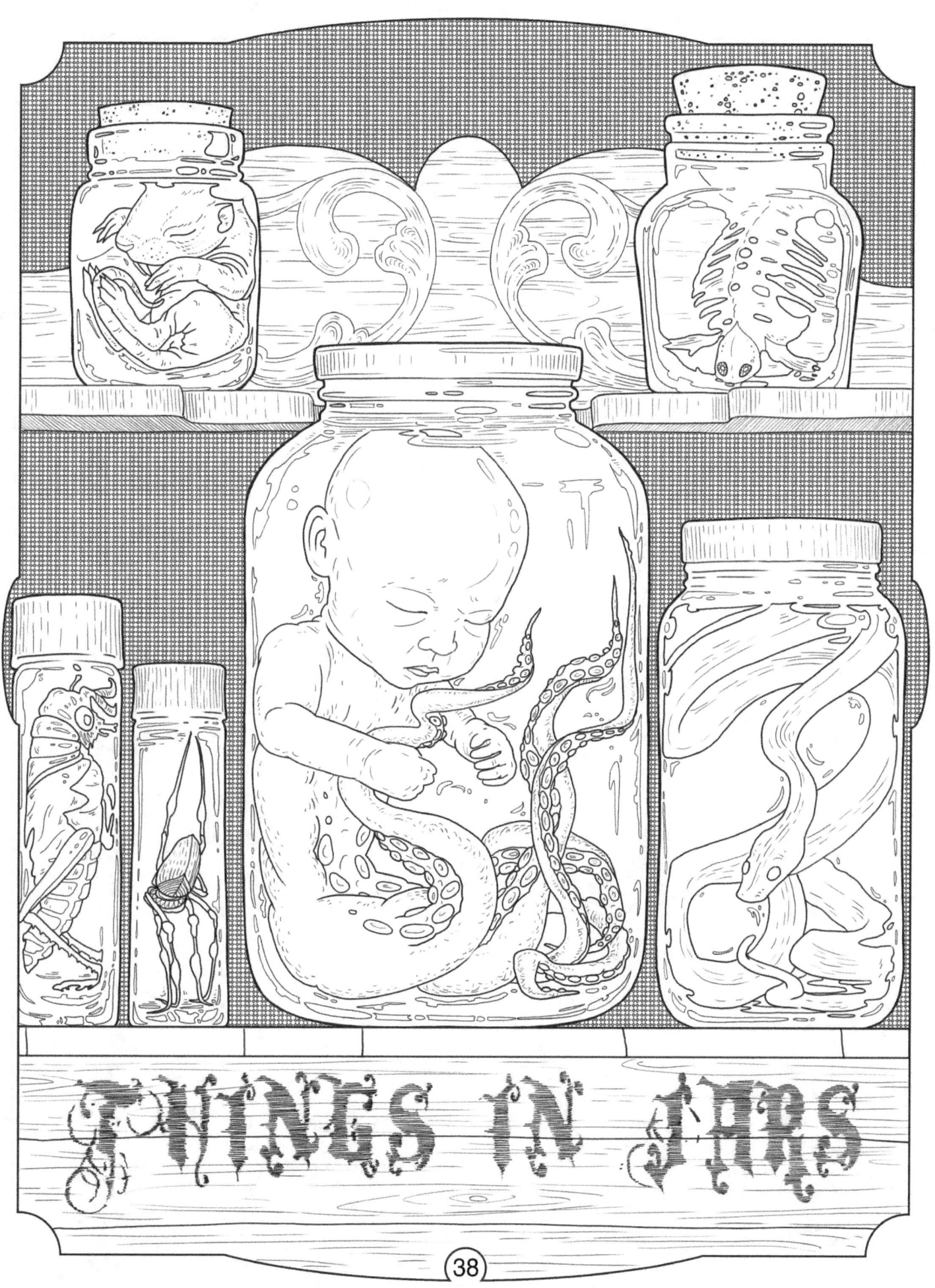

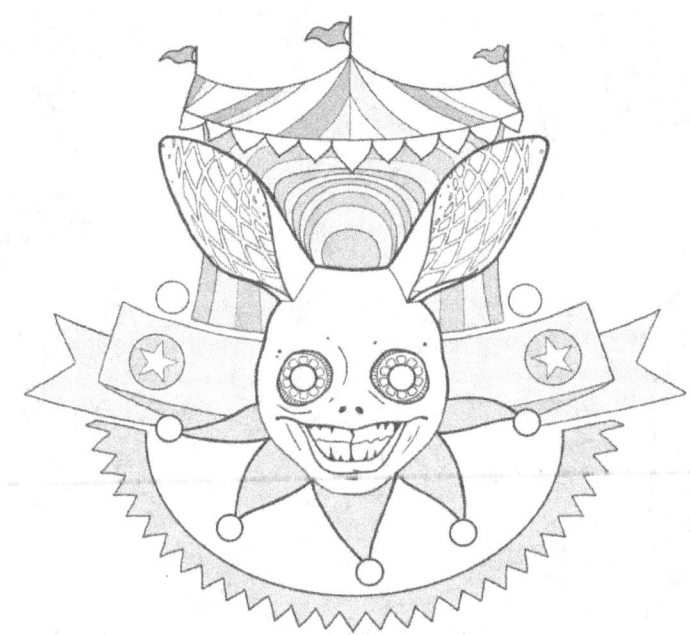

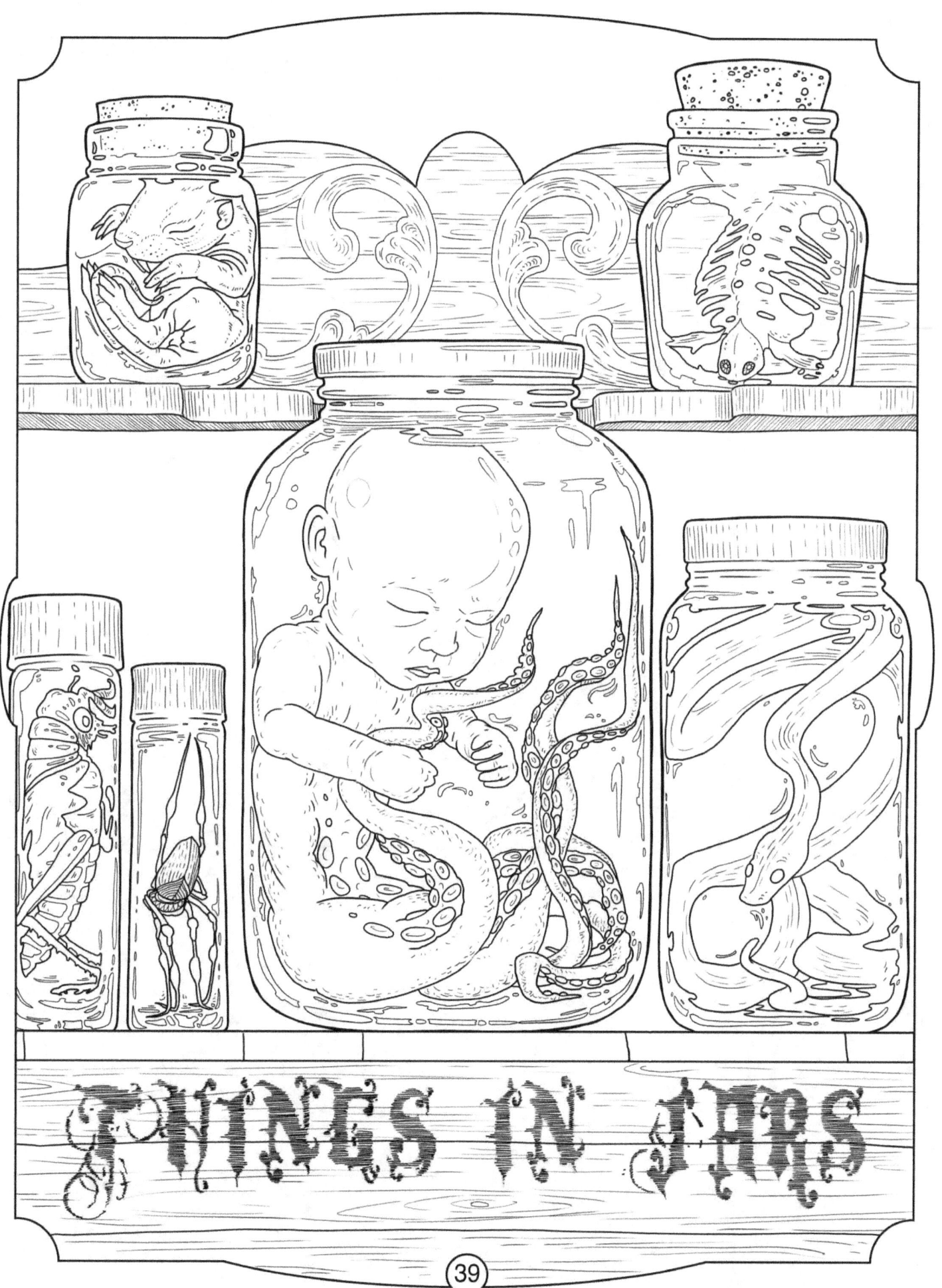

THINGS IN JARS

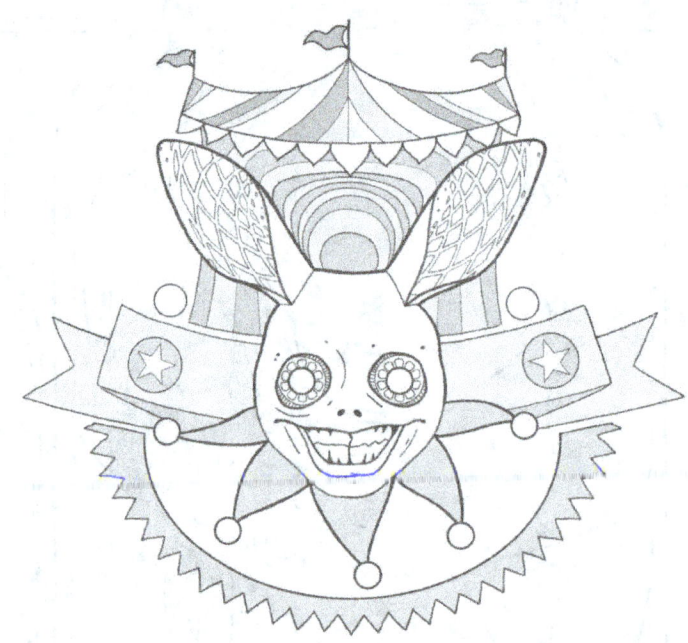

MY OTHER PUBLISHED WORKS

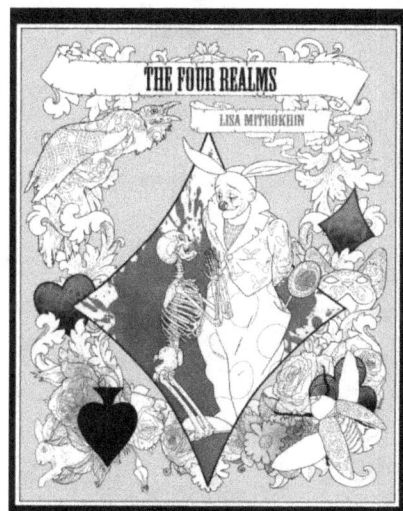

THE FOUR REALMS

8.5" x 11" (21.59 x 27.94 cm)
84 pages
ISBN-13: 978-1546702863
ISBN-10: 1546702865

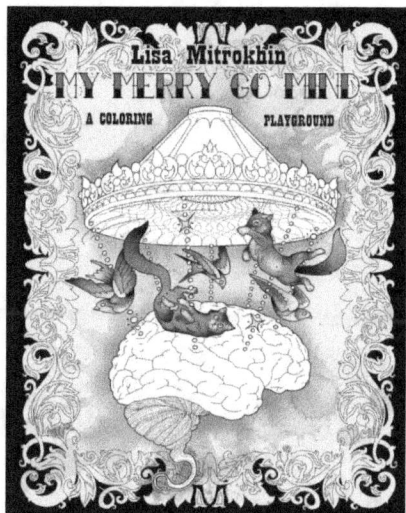

MY MERRY GO MIND

8.5" x 11" (21.59 x 27.94 cm)
74 pages
ISBN-13: 978-1974263196
ISBN-10: 1974263193

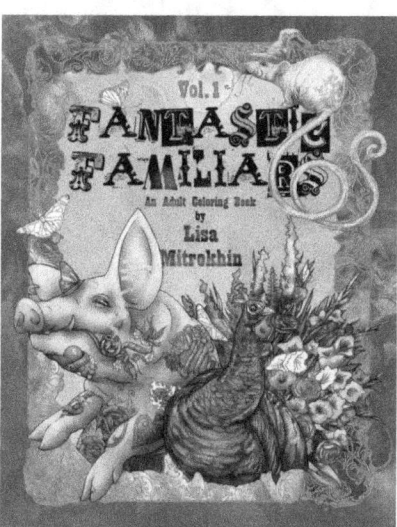

FANTASTIC FAMILIARS (VOL1)

8.5" x 11" (21.59 x 27.94 cm)
84 pages
ISBN-13: 978-1979869553
ISBN-10: 1979869553

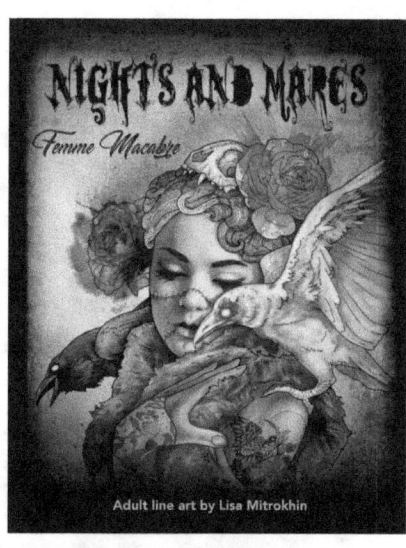

**NIGHTS AND MARES
(FEMME MACABRE)**

8.5" x 11" (21.59 x 27.94 cm)
48 pages
ISBN-13: 978-1984377661
ISBN-10: 1984377663

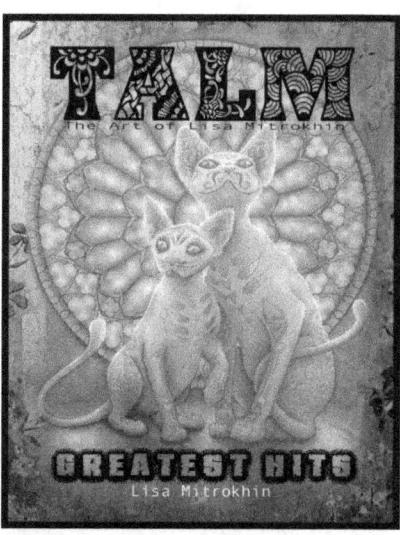

**TALM - THE ART OF
LISA MITROKHIN
GREATEST HITS**

8.5" x 11" (21.59 x 27.94 cm)
62 pages
ISBN-13: 978-1987563597
ISBN-10: 198756359X

For complete flip-throughs of all my books, please visit my website

www.mitrokh.in

All of these books are available on amazon.com

To join my Facebook group and gain access to newly released free pages, visit
https://www.facebook.com/groups/lisamitrokhin/

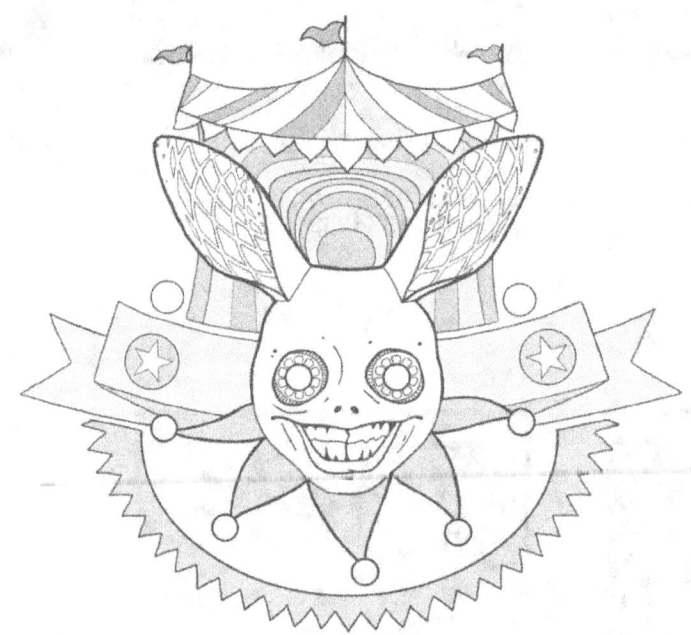

www.ingramcontent.com/pod-product-compliance
Lightning Source LLC
Chambersburg PA
CBHW081613220526
45468CB00010B/2857